ABOUT THE AUTHORS

Tony Fahey is a Research Officer at the Economic and Social Research Institute. He received his undergraduate and Master's level training in the National University of Ireland (Maynooth College) and his Ph.D. in sociology from the University of Illinois at Urbana-Champaign in the USA. He has published extensively on various aspects of the family in Ireland, as well as on the topics of religion (with special reference to Catholicism in Ireland) the elderly and social inclusion.

Maureen Lyons was formerly a Research Assistant at the ESRI. She is now a doctoral student in sociology in Queen's University, Belfast. She received her Bachelor's and Master's degrees in University College Dublin. Her Master's Thesis consisted of a study of the 1986 divorce referendum.

Marital Breakdown and Family Law in Ireland

A Sociological Study

Tony Fahey
Maureen Lyons

Oak Tree Press
Dublin
in association with
The Economic and Social Research Institute

Oak Tree Press
Merrion Building
Lower Merrion Street
Dublin 2, Ireland

© 1995 Tony Fahey and Maureen Lyons

A catalogue record of this book is
available from the British Library

ISBN 1-86076-009-0

Printed in Ireland by Colour Books Ltd.

CONTENTS

LIST OF TABLES

LIST OF FIGURES

PREFACE

The idea for the research on which this study is based dates from 1990. It was initially prompted by a desire to examine the practical workings of the Judicial Separation and Family Law Reform Act 1989, which, when enacted, represented a major departure in Irish family law and was presented as the centrepiece of the legal response to marital breakdown in Ireland.

Lack of research funds meant that the project remained no more than an idea for a number of years. In October 1993, the Justice Commission of the Conference of Religious of Ireland (CORI) offered the ESRI a modest amount of funding to support research on the family in Ireland.[1] This offer was prompted in part by a brief discussion of the absence of such research which had taken place in September 1993 at the annual social policy conference of the CORI (some comments which formed part of that discussion are contained in Fahey, 1993, pp. 128-9).

Faced with this welcome offer, we focused afresh on the idea of research on family law and developed it into a proposal for the present project. By then, we had learned enough about the family law system in Ireland to doubt that the 1989 Act, important though it was, was as central or dominant in the system as we had at first thought. The large numbers of applications for barring orders in the family law business of the courts were especially striking. This feature of the system meant that

---

[1] The CORI is the umbrella organisation of the main religious orders and congregations of the Roman Catholic church in Ireland. Prior to 1994, it was known as the Conference of Major Religious Superiors (CMRS). Within the CORI, the funding for the present project was provided to the Justice Commission by the Southern Province of the Irish Christian Brothers.

protection of spouses and children against violence appeared to
be as significant a focus of family law practice as separation
proceedings in the more usual sense. Family law in Ireland
thus appeared to be dominated by two distinct functions —
marital separation and protection against violence. In addition, proceedings involving non-marital partners seemed to occupy a growing, though still minority, position in the system.
In order to explore these patterns, our concerns shifted from a
focus solely on the 1989 Act to a broader set of questions about
what the main parts of the family law system were, how they
fitted together and what the resulting entity amounted to as a
response to family conflict.

As we spell out further in Chapter One, the study which we
proposed in order to pursue these concerns was of modest proportions. It was designed to sketch in some answers rather
than to provide a comprehensive picture. The limited nature of
the project in part reflected the relatively small scale of the
funding that was available. In addition, sociological research
on family law is a new and undeveloped field of enquiry in
Ireland. It seemed prudent, therefore, to begin with a modest
study and on the basis of what we learned in this first investigation, to think again at a later date about a more extensive
exploration of the field.

When we presented our proposal to the CORI as a possible
target for their funding, it may not have been quite what they
had anticipated. However, after some reflection they agreed to
accept it and contracted to support it on the usual conditions of
independence in the conduct of ESRI research. It should be
said that, having accepted the broad outlines of the project, the
CORI neither asked for nor were offered any subsequent say
on the conduct of the project nor any influence on the content
of the present study. Neither did they ask for or obtain access
to the data collected for the study, other than what is available
to any reader who cares to pick his or her way through the
present text.

The study we designed relied heavily on the collection of
data based on solicitors' family law case-files, and thus required extensive co-operation from solicitors. To enable solicitors to provide that co-operation, the project needed approval

and support from the Incorporated Law Society of Ireland. We therefore approached the Family Law Committee of the Law Society for advice and assistance, both of which were given freely and generously. Following extensive discussion and refinement of the methodology of the study, the Family Law Committee declared itself satisfied that the project was worthwhile and that the data collection in which solicitors were to be asked to participate conformed to necessary standards in regard to solicitors' professional practice and the protection of clients' confidentiality. It recommended the project to the Council of the Law Society on that basis and the Council adopted that recommendation. This cleared the way for the Family Law Committee to inform solicitors that they could participate in the study without infringing their professional responsibilities. The Committee also helped us in identifying and contacting solicitors who might be asked to participate in the study (the details we set out further below and in the Appendix).

All this negotiation and preparatory work had taken over a year to complete, so that it was not until November 1994 that the starting line proper in the research was reached. Fieldwork was completed mainly in December 1994 and January 1995. Analysis of the data and writing of the present study took place between then and June 1995.

Before turning, in the chapters which follow, to the substance of the analysis, we should acknowledge the support and encouragement from others which made it possible to carry the project through. The first and most important support came from the CORI, initially in the shape of their offer of funding and subsequently in the form of encouragement with the work. We thank all the members of that organisation for their help. Seán Healy of the Justice Commission of the CORI was especially important in mediating between us and the CORI, and we gratefully acknowledge his enthusiasm for the project. After the CORI, the next major prop of the study was provided by the Family Law Committee of the Law Society. We thank especially Moya Quinlan (chairperson of the Committee), Joan O'Mahony, Eugene Davy and Pauline O'Reilly. Special mention is due to Linda Kirwan, secretary to the Family Law

Committee, through whom much of the discussions with the Committee passed and who provided a good deal of efficient spadework in helping us with numerous details of the project.

The staff of the Legal Aid Board, in particular Frank Brady, provided assistance of a similar kind in organising the participation of the solicitors in their Law Centres around the country. Joseph Brennan, Chief Examiner of the Department of Justice, not only provided us with statistics on court procedures, some of which took some effort to assemble, but also was patient and helpful in explaining the nature and limitations of those statistics. John Molloy, Deputy Chief Clerk of the Dublin Metropolitan District court, was extraordinarily helpful in arranging with the staff of the court that they would assist us with data collection which we could not have carried out ourselves. The work in compiling the data was carried out efficiently and beyond the call of duty by Court Registrars Rose O'Sullivan, Hilda McDermott and Elisha D'Arcy. The Survey Unit of the ESRI, under the direction of Maura Cagney, provided the fieldwork staff and administration for the survey of solicitors' case files. Enda Bergin provided valuable research assistance at a late stage of the research. We thank all of them for their efficient work.

A number of people gave us valuable comments on earlier drafts of the study. In particular, Dorothy Watson, Mary Bradley and Peter Murray provided thorough and illuminating critical readings. Emer Smyth, Kieran Kennedy and the combined membership of the Family Law Committee of the Law Society also suggested numerous improvements and corrections of fact. Máire Ní Annracháin provided continuous support and encouragement in the course of the work and suggested a number of valuable points about presentation. David Givens of Oak Tree Press saw the book through to publication quickly, calmly and with great professionalism.

Finally, we should say a word about the 87 solicitors who contributed to the data collection. We had been concerned in advance of the project that it might prove difficult to persuade busy solicitors to give of their working time in order to help out with data collection. This concern proved unfounded: unusually for such a project, the refusal rate from those we contacted for information was almost zero. Solicitors seemed eager to co-operate, not only out of a spirit of helpfulness but out of a hope that this project might help throw light on a field of practice that is rapidly growing, is largely new to many solicitors and often involves harrowing family circumstances that they can find difficult to come to terms with. We took encouragement from the very positive response of solicitors to the project and we hope the result will be worthy of the help they gave us.

CHAPTER 1

NATURE OF STUDY

Background

Controversy about divorce has long kept the family law system
at the centre of public debate in Ireland. Yet, apart from some
pioneering work by Ward (1990, 1993), no real attempt has
been made to find out how the system works in practice or how
it relates to the daily realities of family life. The result is an
extraordinary level of ignorance about the social dimensions of
family law.[1] This arises not only in connection with the large,
difficult questions which have proved impossible to answer
simply or conclusively in any country — why marital breakdown has increased so much, what effect legal divorce has on
families, especially on children, what effect changes in family
law have on marital stability. More significantly, it arises in
connection with simpler questions about the nuts and bolts of
the existing family law system in Ireland — how many people
make use of the system, who those people are, what kinds of
family conflicts they ask the law to deal with, what solutions
the system offers them, what, in overall outline, the system
looks like.

These are straightforward questions, but they have never
been asked in Ireland. One might expect that the answers
would be essential if any major changes in family law, such as
the introduction of divorce, were to be contemplated — how
can we think of adding on a major new wing to a structure we
know so little about? Yet there has been an almost studied de-

---

[1] The legal dimensions have been set out more thoroughly — see especially
Shatter (1986), O'Connor (1988) and Duncan and Scully (1990). For an earlier, socially-oriented study, see O'Higgins (1974).

sire to avoid them. This is so not only at the level of public debate, where much of the controversy about divorce has an air of unreality, given that it is sometimes better informed about marital breakdown and the legal response in America or Britain than in Ireland.

More worryingly, it is also true among legislators and official policy-makers. The poor standard of knowledge at this level can be seen in the inadequacy of official monitoring statistics on the family law system. These statistics provide little information on the elementary facts of the system — how many family law cases arise each year, how many go to court and how many are resolved by agreement outside of court, how many have a history of repeated recourse to the law, how many involve children, what the social and family circumstances of the litigants are, what kinds of decisions the courts offer, how far these decisions are put into effect, and so on. As we shall see later, the statistics do tell us that domestic violence plays a very large role in family law cases appearing before the courts in Ireland but they stop short at that. They tell us nothing about the nature of the violence (how often it is psychological rather than physical, how repetitive it is, how severe it is), about the victims and perpetrators (we do not know, for example, how often children as well as women are victims), about the kinds of responses the courts give (we do not know, for example, why more than half the barring applications made in 1993-94 were not granted), about the pattern of enforcement of orders issued, about rates of recidivism, or about any other practical outcome as far as families are concerned.

This lack of elementary factual knowledge carries through into the poor information base for official policy analysis as far as the social aspects of family law are concerned. The major policy documents on family law of recent years, such as the *Report on the Joint Committee on Marriage Breakdown* (1985) and *Marital Breakdown: A Review and Proposed Changes* (Department of Justice, 1992), have lacked systematic empirical investigation or analysis of the social aspects of their subject matter. The Law Reform Commission, which has produced a number of important documents on family law reform (esp.

Law Reform Commission, 1994), has no remit to commission or carry out socio-legal research. Likewise, the Department of Equality and Law Reform has been assigned the responsibility for the reform of family law since 1993 without any backup social research function. The only instance of a public sector agency giving substantial support for socially-oriented research in this area that we are aware of is the Combat Poverty Agency's support for Peter Ward's work on the financial consequences of marital breakdown (Ward, 1990).

In short, as far as the social dimension of family law is concerned, legislators and policy makers have been driving in the dark, or at least with very poor lights, and seem neither to have the desire nor the means to examine the social context or social impact of what they are doing. In this area, they have been content to make and change law without conducting systematic research into how the law works in practice or in what areas it can and should be made to work better.

Aims of the Study

This publication is intended as a modest contribution to this largely undeveloped field. The study on which it is based was constrained by its limited research resources and therefore confined itself to the basic task of describing, from a sociological perspective, some of the main features of the family law system in Ireland. It attempts to answer a number of basic questions, principally as follows:

- What are the main types of cases processed by the Irish family law system?

- Who are the clients who take those cases — what are the social and family circumstances of those who have recourse to the law as a remedy for family conflict?

- What issues do clients seek to have addressed by the family law system — what aspects of their family arrangements do they ask the family law system to deal with?

- What are the legal outcomes of family law cases — what remedies does the family law system offer those who have recourse to it?

On the basis of the information the study assembles on these questions, it also tries to draw certain limited conclusions on the question of the level and trend of marital breakdown in Ireland. We should also say that it had been our original intention to focus in some detail on the place of children in family law cases. In the event, we did gather some basic information on this issue. However, children proved to be less evident in family law cases than one might expect, to the extent that their comparative *absence* from our data sources proved to be a significant item of information in itself. We return briefly to the implications of this fact in the concluding chapter.

The study makes no attempt to explore larger questions about family conflict — for example, the causes and consequences of increased marital breakdown, or the impact of legal changes on the institution of marriage. These are important issues but they cannot be treated properly within such a limited study as this.

Scope of the Study

In order to identify what we mean by family law cases and thus to define the scope of the present study, we focused on contact with solicitors and District Court clerks as entry points into the system and thus as boundary markers of family law cases. Anyone who wishes to have recourse to family law usually has to approach either a solicitor or a District Court clerk in order to get the relevant processes under way. In that sense, solicitors and District Court clerks perform a doorkeeper function in the family law system. For the purposes of this study, we consider that a family law case comes into being when one of the parties in a family conflict requests either a solicitor or a District Court clerk to take action on his or her behalf. By "action" here we include a range of things — the issuing of proceedings for a court hearing, the opening of negotiations by a solicitor aimed at an out-of-court settlement, or the compilation or drafting of legal documents. The giving of advice on its own does not constitute action in this sense. Solicitors are frequently approached by clients who want advice and information on their rights and the options open to them in family law but who do not subsequently instruct the solicitor to take action on their behalf.[2] Cases come within the ambit of our study when the client involved "instructs" his or her solicitor to take some action rather than when he or she merely consults the solicitor for advice or information. The study focuses on family law cases so defined, and circumscribes the family law system by reference to the laws and legal institutions (particularly the courts and legal professions) which routinely come into play in dealing with those cases.

Mediation

This way of defining the target of the study means that we largely excluded mediation proceedings from its remit (mediation is often referred to as conciliation, and we use the two terms interchangeably here). In mediation, the partners jointly request a professional mediator (who usually is not a solicitor) to help them work out an agreement to settle the practical consequences of the breakdown of their marriage.[3] Mediation is increasingly being advocated as a valuable means of arriving at legal settlement of family conflicts, mainly on the grounds that settlements which are worked out by negotiation and agreement between the partners are more likely to be accepted and less likely to engender further stress and bitterness than are adversarial court proceedings. Mediated agreements are also usually thought to have an advantage over out-of-

---

[2] In the civil legal aid service, for example, over half of the family law cases dealt with consist of advice only (Legal Aid Board, 1993)

[3] "Mediation proceeds from the premise that the marriage has broken down and seeks to promote agreement between the parties on specific legal and practical issues such as child custody, property matters and maintenance" (Law Reform Commission, 1994, p. 32). It differs from *reconciliation*, which aims to repair a damaged marriage so that it can continue or resume, and from *counselling*, which involves professional help with emotional and psychological problems either among individuals or couples.

court agreements negotiated between solicitors on the grounds that a single non-partisan mediator, who is professionally trained to find common ground between conflicting partners, is more likely to achieve mutually acceptable and durable agreements than adversarial solicitors whose training and professional ethos gears them to seeking one-sided advantage for whichever side of the conflict they represent.[4]

Some research has been carried out on family mediation in Ireland (Nic Ghiolla Phádraig, 1992) and it would have been useful to include it within the scope of the present study. However, we did not do so, mainly because it would have added a major additional dimension to the study. In addition, we were likely in any event to get some information on mediation through solicitors' case files. Spouses who arrive at a separation agreement through mediation usually take the agreement to their respective solicitors for legal fine-tuning and for final drafting into a deed of separation. Such mediated settlements are represented in the present study, and can be identified as such, through the resulting solicitor's case-files — though we do not have enough information to tell how much of the work on such cases was conducted through mediation and how much through solicitors. However, we cannot say anything about mediation cases which did not eventually reach a solicitor.

For present purposes, therefore, we have in effect treated mediation as preliminary or adjunct to family law proceedings rather than as an internal component. We get a sidelong glance at mediation in those cases where it ties into the family law system through the use of solicitor's services, but we do not deal with it directly. This is not to say that mediation actually is of marginal importance — the opposite is the case — but rather that, for practical reasons, it is necessary to set it largely to one side in the present study.

---

[4] In practice, solicitors may often temper their advocacy of their client's interests in order to achieve what they would consider a fair and sensible outcome for both parties. However, neither by training nor professional obligation are solicitors geared to non-partisan negotiation, so that, in contrast with mediators, they can modify their adversarial stance towards the other side in a dispute only to a limited extent.

Informal Separation

The focus on family law cases means that the scope of the study does not extend to informal separation, that is, marital separation which occurs without reference to family law. In informal separation, spouses cease to live together but otherwise seek neither legal separation nor any other more specific legal remedy such as a maintenance award, a custody or access order or a barring order. The nature of their separation may be influenced by the law — for example, by what they expect would be the outcome if they did have recourse to law, or by an unwillingness to risk the stress and acrimony which a legal case might bring on — but it does not directly involve legal action. As we shall see further below in Chapter Six, informal separation in this sense may account for a substantial share of all marital breakdowns in Ireland, but precise information is lacking. In other words, family law cases as we define them form only a sub-set of marital breakdowns but we do not really know what the gap in numbers is between the two.

Marital Conflict

Within the family law case load as we define it, our main focus is on conflict between spouses or between those who have been involved in non-marital sexual relationships (with or without cohabitation). We often refer to this type of conflict as "marital" conflict. Strictly speaking, this term is a misnomer since the scope of the study includes conflicts between cohabiting partners, and even between men and women who have had sexual relationships without ever cohabiting. Both these kinds of relationships have become sufficiently common in Irish social life for us to have an interest in the degree to which they surface in family law proceedings. A more inclusive label for our target area, then, would be "partnership conflicts". However, since this is a neologism which has no currency in Ireland, we will avoid it in favour of the more familiar if less adequate "marital conflict", while keeping in mind the non-marital conflicts we want to include under that heading.

We exclude those aspects of family law which are not normally linked to marital or partnership conflict (such as adop-

tion law, the law relating to contracting marriage and most of
the law of inheritance). By focusing on civil law, we exclude
those aspects of the criminal law which are often applied to
conflicts within families (such as the law relating to rape
within marriage, child abuse or the breaches of barring orders
by barred spouses).[5] Furthermore, we concentrate on the commonly used procedures in family law, so that we do not attempt to examine in any detail those which occur too rarely to
figure prominently in a sample study such as the present one
(thus, for example, we make little reference to family law cases
in the High Court).

It is clear from the limitations just set out that we do not
attempt to examine all interactions between families and the
law. However, the sub-set we do focus on — the main range of
legal procedures which partners in marriage or marriage-like
relationships commonly have recourse to as a means of resolv-
ing conflicts in their relationships (including conflicts over
their respective rights and obligations in relation to their children) — is clearly important and can reasonably be treated as
a meaningful entity for research purposes.

Legally Unrepresented Cases

Having defined the scope of the study in the terms just outlined, we found in practice that certain areas within it were
easier to cover than others. The main problem arose in connection with those cases which clients initiate and follow
through by approaching District Court clerks without legal
representation. In these cases, applicants ask District Court
clerks to issue proceedings on their behalf, as clerks are empowered to do.[6] While some applicants who initiate proceedings in this way subsequently engage a solicitor to represent
them in court, many do not. In the latter instance, the cases
proceed to hearings in the District Court (or are abandoned by
the applicant, as often happens) and are concluded without the

---

[5] See "Barring Procedures" in Chapter Two.

[6] Under the Family Law (Maintenance of Spouses and Children) Act, 1976
and the District Court Rules made thereunder.

involvement of solicitors. Though the substance of these cases can often be quite serious, many of them have only a fleeting contact with the family law system and are documented only in a minimal way.

For example, a woman in the Dublin area applying for a protection and barring order might initiate her action by appearing at the Dublin Metropolitan District court offices on a given morning (see pp. 20-21 below, where the nature of protection and barring procedures is outlined). She would have a brief interview with a District Court clerk and perhaps within an hour have a hearing of the protection application in the District judge's chambers. Some days or weeks later she might return for what could well be a rather perfunctory hearing of the barring application. In many cases, the woman might have no legal representation at any point in the proceedings and her husband might neither turn up in court nor be legally represented. The application would be likely to allege serious misconduct on the husband's part (such as violence against his wife) and could well have massive implications for the family, whether granted or not. However, by comparison with many other family law proceedings, particularly those conducted in the stricter and more formal atmosphere of the Circuit Court, the legal processing of the case could be quite brief (cf. Duncan and Scully, 1990, p. 106).

Since solicitors do not become involved in such cases, the information and documentation which solicitors would normally compile in representing clients is absent. Records of these cases are kept in District Court files but these records contain only the barest information, consisting mainly of the names and addresses of the applicant and respondent, the nature of the application and the ensuing order or orders issued by the court. This information has been mined more or less to its limit in previous research (Ward, 1988, 1990) but it is too narrow and too difficult to access to be of much value for the questions of concern to us here. In many instances, relevant documentation may be compiled in other arenas — by social workers or community welfare officers in the Health Boards, for example — but even where such documentation exists the linkages are not there to allow the researcher to connect it with District Court files. These cases are further hidden to research by the *in camera* rules which restrict third party access to family law hearings, meaning, among other things, that researchers such as ourselves cannot routinely attend the hearings of such cases in court. All of this is added to by the general over-burdening of the District Court system which forces it to process large volumes of family law business with often minimal scrutiny of individual cases, and which makes it difficult for highly pressurised court officials to deal with the kind of research queries we sometimes directed at them in the course of the present project.

Legally unrepresented cases, then, constitute what, from a research point of view, could be regarded as a large, almost subterranean body of family law practice within the family law system. Had our resources been generous enough, it would have been possible (though difficult) to compile a sample of such half-hidden cases and gather information about them directly from the litigants themselves. However, we did not have the resources to search out or deal directly with litigants, so that option was ruled out. Rather than abandon this area of family law practice entirely in the study, we attempted to collect certain basic items of information on a small sample of family law cases through court officials in the Dublin Metropolitan District (DMD) Court, if only to establish how common such legally unrepresented cases were. The resulting information was limited and somewhat uncertain in quality (see below). However, it did indicate that 55 per cent of applicants and 56 per cent of respondents in the District Court sample had no legal representation on the day their case was heard in court. On this admittedly limited evidence, therefore, it appears that unrepresented family law cases amount to something of the order of half the family law cases in the District Court.

This suggests, then, that legally unrepresented cases form a large and highly significant part of the family law system and should be taken into account in any overall assessment of the social role of family law. From our sample of DMD Court cases, we can offer some scraps of knowledge on this segment of the system but little more than that. We cannot say definitively how significant the resulting gap is since so little is known about the scale or importance of what we have omitted.

Given the marginalisation of legally unrepresented family law cases in the study, its main focus is on family law cases that pass through the hands of solicitors. Solicitors are key agents in the family law system, in that apart from the cases just mentioned which are initiated through District Court clerks, practically all other cases are initiated through them and are followed through with their legal advice and representation. The solicitor's function is much more extensive and pivotal than that of District Court clerks, since they advise and represent clients and, where necessary, brief barristers as well as issue proceedings.[7] Furthermore, many family law cases which are initiated through solicitors are settled by agreement without going to court, usually with solicitors for the two sides taking part in, if not leading, the negotiation process which leads to agreement. Such negotiated settlements are then formalised through deeds of separation (separation agreements) or other agreements drawn up by solicitors. In other words, for many family law litigants, their solicitors *are* the family law system as far as their contact with the system is concerned.[8]

In summary, then, the scope of the present study is limited very much to family law cases which are processed with the help of solicitors. We retain throughout an interest in the extent and nature of family law cases that are taken without the services of solicitors in the District Courts, but these remain

---

[7] District Court clerks also often play a significant role in advising those clients who request them to issue proceedings in family law cases on their behalf. However, the Clerks' advisory role, while important in practice, has no formal standing. Their prescribed role is as administrators of court business so that any advisory function they perform is informal and fleeting rather than a formally defined function.

[8] In order to give a separation agreement extra legal force, the parties to it may apply to have it made a rule of court. This does not affect the content of the agreement but means that if one side breaches the agreement, the breach can be treated as a contempt of court rather than as a civil matter between the two sides. This increases the enforceability of the agreement.

very much a *terra incognito* which we can do little more than speculate about on the basis of very little hard information.

Data Sources

Two original data sources are used for the present study. The first and principal one is a survey of 87 solicitors which collected information on 510 of their family law cases (that is, an average of almost six cases per solicitor). One hundred and fifty-three of these cases were taken from solicitors employed by the Legal Aid Board while the remaining 357 were taken from solicitors in private practice. This division of the sample between private and Legal Aid solicitors was intended to be representative of national patterns but, because of lack of information on national patterns in this area, we cannot say how far it does so (see Appendix I for details). For each sampled case, solicitors were interviewed by ESRI interviewers in order to obtain general socio-demographic information on the client and the client's partner, an outline of the legally relevant substance of the case and information on the outcome of the case as far as maintenance, the disposition of the family home and children were concerned. Solicitor's supplied this information by consulting the case-file records which they held on each case, as well as by drawing on their own knowledge and recollections of the case. We will refer to this source throughout the study as the *solicitors' case-file sample*.

The second data source arises from a limited attempt to get some basic information on legally unrepresented family law cases in the District Court. It is based on a sample of 132 family law cases in the family court (Dolphin House) in the Dublin Metropolitan District (DMD). The information obtained on these cases was provided by Court Registrars on a standardised recording form which Registrars completed as the sample cases came up for hearing in the court on a selection of days in the period December 1994 to February 1995. We refer to this source throughout the study as the *DMD Court sample*.

A full account of how both of these information sources were compiled is contained in Appendix I.

In addition to these original data sources, we also draw on statistics of court procedures in family law supplied to us by the Department of Justice. These statistics are analysed in detail in Chapter Two below.

None of this information was collected from the main actors in family law cases — the family members themselves — but from solicitors or officials familiar with those cases. In a certain sense, therefore, the information we use is second-hand. It gives a less personal insight into the realities of family conflict and its interaction with family law than would be provided by the main actors, particularly if both main actors could be interviewed. We stopped short of interviews with main actors in family law cases almost entirely for reasons of economy. Furthermore, while many family law cases involve two opposing solicitors (one for each side in the case), we interviewed the solicitor for one side only and made no attempt to gather corroborating or additional information from the opposing solicitor. While interviews with both solicitors would have been useful in many ways, we did not consider the work and cost involved to be the best way of using scarce research resources.

While the data do have limitations, therefore, they also have strengths, particularly in the case of the solicitors' casefile sample. Solicitors' case-files usually contain documentation (in the form of interview notes, letters, copies of legal documents, etc.) which record the family circumstances of family law clients, the legal substance of their cases and, where cases are concluded or nearly so, the legal outcome of the case. Given that we focus on current or recently concluded cases which were fresh in solicitors' memories at the time of interview, the solicitor's own recollections can add detail and background to the documentary record. Case-file data may be weak on the personal and emotional dimension of family conflicts or on the deeper family background from which they emerged, but they provide good quality information on those more immediate issues which are the concern of the present study. Despite the many large gaps, therefore, the information drawn from this source can illuminate aspects of the family law system which are important for policy and which have been little investigated to date.

Structure of Study

Following this introductory chapter, the study is presented in six further chapters. Chapter Two examines general patterns in the family law caseload appearing before the courts by means of annual statistics on court procedures compiled by the Department of Justice. This chapter also examines trends over time and regional patterns in the family law caseload. Chapter Three turns to the solicitors' case-file to provide a social profile of solicitors' family law clients. Chapter Four deals with the legal substance of the sampled cases — how they were initiated, what the points at issue were and what legal procedures were pursued. Chapter Five focuses on concluded cases in the sample and asks what the legal outcomes were. Chapter Six turns to the debate concerning the quantification of marital breakdown rates in Ireland and makes a number of estimates which may help clarify this question. Chapter Seven draws out the conclusions and implications of the study. It focuses especially on a number of dualisms found in the practical workings of the Irish family law system and offers some observations on the issues and implications these pose for family law reform in Ireland.

CHAPTER 2

NATIONAL FAMILY LAW CASELOAD

Introduction

In most western countries, the practice of family law has grown rapidly over recent decades. Marital conflict and divorce have been the main driving force in that growth, with the result that in most western countries proceedings for divorce and related issues dominate the business of family courts. There has been some growth in the law relating to non-marital partnerships or cohabitation (including, in some jurisdictions, same-sex partnerships). However, while the legal conception of the family has been thereby expanded somewhat, litigation between non-married partners still seems to occupy a relatively small place in the family law systems of most western countries (Goode, 1993).

Irish family law does not allow for divorce, yet this has not stopped the practice of family law from growing in this country too, especially since the early 1980s. As in other countries, marital conflict and marital breakdown have provided the main impetus for the growth of family law practice in Ireland. Irish law has abundant provisions relating to marital breakdown which would be counted as branches or adjuncts of divorce law in other countries — provisions for maintenance, custody and access, division of property, legal separation and so on — and it is this assortment of provisions which has provided much of the legal framework for the growth of family law practice in Ireland. Irish family law also has important provisions relating to the protection of spouses and children against violence which, as we shall see further below, accounts for a strikingly large portion of family law business in the courts. In addition, there is some increase in the possibility of legal proceedings involving non-married partners, at least where the partnership in question has resulted in the birth of children. The Status of Children Act, 1987, which abolished most of the legal distinction between marital and non-marital children, was an important legal departure in this regard and has greatly expanded this area of family law practice in the courts.

Despite the absence of divorce, therefore, the Irish family law system has a well-developed character. The purpose of this chapter is to explore the annual statistics on family law proceedings in the Irish courts complied by the Department of Justice in order to get a preliminary view of what that character is. We will refer also to data from our DMD Court sample in order to illuminate certain aspects of the Department of Justice statistics. We will confine our attention to the District Court and Circuit Court, since the numbers of family law cases appearing before the High Court are comparatively small.[1]

From these sources we will be able to indicate the main types of family law cases appearing before the courts and the frequency with which they occur. As we shall see, the information we can glean is not always clear-cut and requires careful examination and interpretation (and, of course, court statistics provide no information on family law cases which are settled out of court, a category of cases which we will deal with from our solicitors' case-file sample in later chapters). Nevertheless, the statistics provide important insight into the structure of the Irish family law system and enables us to set the context for the subsequent chapters of the present study.

Statistics on Court Proceedings

Table 2.1 presents national statistics for District Court and Circuit Court family law proceedings for the legal year from

---

[1] Apart from appeals from the Circuit Court, on which no data are available, the main family law proceedings to appear before the High Court are applications for civil nullity. There were 72 such applications in 1993-94, of which 23 were granted. In addition, separation proceedings are sometimes initiated at High Court level, usually in cases involving land with a rateable valuation in excess of £200 (see Section 31.3 of the 1989 Act). There were 41 applications for judicial separation in the High Court in 1993-94, of which 21 were granted (data supplied by Department of Justice).

August 1993 to July 1994. The nature of these statistics differs for the two court levels and they do not provide full coverage of family law proceedings. Before we attempt to decipher what they mean, we need to consider at some length what kinds of information they contain.

Table 2.1: Court Procedures in Family Law for Year Ending 31 July 1994

	Number of Applications	Orders Granted	
		Number	As % of Applications
District Court			
Maintenance	2,943	2,241	76
Barring	4,457	2,010	45
Protection	3,091	n/a	n/a
Guardianship	3,665	n/a	n/a
Protection of Family Home	67	n/a	n/a
Paternity test*	51	n/a	n/a
Total	**14,274**	n/a	n/a
Circuit Court			
Judicial separation	2,806	986	35

* Under Section 38, Status of Children Act, 1987
Source: Department of Justice

The statistics for the District Court are the most detailed, in that separate counts are given for each of the main family law procedures applied for in the District Courts — maintenance, barring, guardianship and so on. No count is given, however, of the number of family law cases or applicants at District Court level. A case may consist of a number of different applications, or may reappear in court with similar applications on more than one occasion, so that the number of cases will be a good deal smaller than the number of applications. Neither is any information given on the social characteristics or family circumstances of applicants. For some procedures in the District Court, counts are given of the number of applications granted, though no details are given on the content of the orders made.

Neither are details available on the reasons for which applications are not granted — for example, whether they were refused or adjourned, and if so on what grounds, or whether they were dismissed because the applicant failed to appear in court on the day of the hearing.

The statistics for the Circuit Court are more limited in that they refer only to applications for judicial separation under the Judicial Separation and Family Law Reform Act, 1989. No counts are given of the ancillary applications (relating to maintenance, property, custody and so on) which might be made under the 1989 Act in conjunction with applications for judicial separation. (The low proportion of applications for judicial separation which are granted, as reported in Table 2.1, probably reflects backlogs in the Circuit System rather than a high refusal rate. This question is discussed further below). Thus, in what is the reverse of the pattern for District Court statistics, the Circuit Court statistics provide a count of judicial separation cases but not of the applications which make these up. This is a major difference in that the 1989 Act is an umbrella statute which allows for a wide range of proceedings to take place under its cover. A further difference from District Court statistics is that repeat counting of cases is much less likely to occur in the Circuit Court statistics. Circuit Court cases tend to be so elaborate and drawn out that successive recurrences of an individual case are unusual.

Circuit Court statistics have a further slight limitation in that they relate only to judicial separation cases, which means that no counts are available of applications or cases which might arise under family legislation other than the 1989 Act, for example barring applications arising under the Family Law (Protection of Children and Spouses) Act, 1981, or maintenance applications under the Family Law (Maintenance of Spouses and Children) Act, 1976. Proceedings of the latter kind occupy a relatively small place in the family law business of the Circuit Court, if only because they tend to be dealt with as part of composite proceedings under the 1989 Act rather than as free-standing applications. However, the lack of reference to them in the data makes for a certain incompleteness in the statistical picture. As with the District Court statistics, counts are given of the number of orders granted by the Court, but again without details of the content of orders and without any information on the circumstances of applications which were not granted.

For the Circuit Court, in short, we could say that the statistics in effect relate principally to cases rather than applications. The District Court statistics, by contrast, give a full count of applications, but no count of cases. Both sets of statistics give counts of orders granted for certain applications but no details either on the content of orders made nor on the reasons for which applications were not granted. The statistics therefore give substantial information on some issues but are sketchy on others. They also differ internally in the nature of the information they provide. They therefore give a picture of family law business in the courts which is useful but less than complete and which is not always easy to interpret.

Structure of Family Law Caseload

Given the nature of the statistics, we have to be careful in attempting to read off the broad structure of the family law caseload in the courts from Table 2.1. Nevertheless, certain patterns do seem to stand out. The first is that the bulk of family law business in the courts arises at District Court level rather than at Circuit Court level. Total applications in the District Court in 1993-94 numbered 14,274 compared to 2,806 applications for judicial separation in the Circuit Court. The difference between the two is inflated in these numbers since, as we have just seen, District Court statistics refer to applications and contain a greater degree of multiple counting of individual cases than do the Circuit Court statistics. We will attempt below to arrive at a rough estimate of the count of cases in the District Court in 1993-94. To anticipate here somewhat, that count probably exceeded 8,000 cases, of which over 5,000 were new ones and the remainder were repeat cases that had been before the courts on previous occasions. It is clear in any event that the number of District Court cases exceeds the number of judicial separation cases in the Circuit Court by a large margin, possibly by as much as two to one. In terms of numbers of cases dealt with in the courts, therefore, the District Court rather than the Circuit Court is the more important locus of family law proceedings in Ireland.

The large volume of family law business in the District Court tells us something about the relative importance of various statutes as reference points for Irish family law practice. Most notably, it suggests that, in terms of sheer numbers of applications to the courts, the Judicial Separation and Family Law Reform Act, 1989 is not the dominant piece of legislation in the Irish family law system. The 1989 Act provides the main statutory basis for the family law business of the Circuit Court and is the relevant legislation for the 2,806 applications made to that court in 1993-94. However, the 1989 Act has no role in the family law jurisdiction of the District Court, so that the considerably larger number of family law cases appearing before that court are covered by other statutes.

Barring Procedures

The breakdown of applications within the District Court gives us an indication of what these statutes are and suggests a second striking feature of the family law caseload — the prominence of barring and protection proceedings. Applications for barring and protection orders are made under the Family Law (Protection of Children and Spouses) Act, 1981. Barring orders provide for the exclusion of a spouse (in practice, usually the husband)[2] from the family home on the grounds that he is guilty of serious misconduct which poses a threat to the safety and welfare of the other spouse and/or their children. Protection orders are interim measures which can be granted immediately when barring proceedings are issued. Their purpose is to secure interim protection for applicants against their

---

[2] In a small minority of cases, husbands are the applicants and women the respondents in barring cases. In our sample of DMD Court cases, of the 51 barring applications 3 were made by men. One of these alleged alcoholism, drug addiction and violence against the wife, the second alleged violence and financial irresponsibility, while in the third details of the allegations were not available.

spouses while they are waiting for a barring application to be heard in court. The protection order does not exclude the spouse from any premises but makes it a criminal offence for him to verbally or physically abuse or threaten his wife in advance of the hearing of the barring application (Duncan and Scully, 1990, p. 94).

Violence is the most common circumstance in which protection and barring orders are granted, but various forms of psychological or verbal degradation or abuse may also be accepted as adequate grounds.[3] The misconduct in question must also be "continuous or repetitive" and "wilful and avoidable". Occasional or once-off acts of misconduct generally would not qualify as a ground for a barring order unless they were of an extreme nature. The maximum term of a barring order in the District Court is twelve months, but it can be renewed by application. At present, barring and protection procedures can be taken only by one spouse against another. Cohabiting partners cannot avail of this procedure, nor can any family members other than spouses. This means that all applicants for protection or barring orders are married and the respondent in all cases is the other spouse.[4]

In 1993-94, 4,457 barring applications were made to the District Court. Applications for protection can be made only in conjunction with barring applications. There were 3,091 protection applications in 1993-94, which means that two-thirds of barring applications were accompanied by protection applications. Of the one-third of barring applications which were not accompanied by protection applications, some may have been repeat or renewal applications where the wife was already protected by an existing barring order. Others may be accounted for as instances where the wife felt under no imme-

---

[3] For a full examination of the grounds for granting barring orders and the rather uncertain precedents concerning their interpretation, see Duncan and Scully (1990, pp. 89-94). See also *Report of the Joint Committee on Marriage Breakdown* (1985, pp. 66-71).

[4] The recently published Domestic Violence Bill proposes to extend the jurisdiction of barring procedures to cover a wider range of forms of domestic violence.

diate threat — for example, where the husband was in prison or was away for a period, or where she had obtained refuge with relatives or in a shelter.

The total of barring applications is remarkably high. It exceeds the number of applications for separation in the Circuit Court by 60 per cent and is higher than the next largest category of applications in the District Court — applications for guardianship[5] — by 22 per cent. It thus can claim to be the largest category of family law business not only in the District Court but at any level of the court system as far as family law is concerned. The prominence of this category also suggests that the protection of women and children against violence at the hands of husbands/fathers is as important a function of the family law system as the regulation of separation in the more usual sense.

Multiple Counting of Barring Cases

Before looking further at the implications of the high incidence of barring procedures, we need to scrutinise the statistics and consider if the count of barring applications in any way falsely enlarges the true picture or gives a misleading impression of the number of family law cases which are centred on spousal violence. The most likely source of distortion in the statistics is multiple counting of cases arising from repeat applications for barring orders from an individual spouse. This can happen when a spouse making a first barring application does not proceed with it (usually by not turning up in court the day the application is heard) and allows it to lapse, but then follows up with a new application at a later date. It can also occur where the term of an earlier barring order has ended and the spouse returns to court to apply for a new order. These patterns would mean that the number of families who have recourse to barring procedures is a good deal less than the number of barring applications made in the courts.

---

[5] That is, applications relating to custody and access to children and the appointment of non-marital fathers as guardians under the Guardianship of Children Act, 1964.

How extensive is such multiple counting? We have no way of answering this question precisely. Anecdotal evidence from family law practitioners and administrators suggests that repeat applications do occur but are not sufficient to account for more than a limited share of the total number of barring applications. The only statistical evidence we have on this question derives from our sample of family law cases in the DMD Court. In that small sample, two out of three applications of all kinds (barring, maintenance, custody and access, etc.) were first applications, while the remaining one out of three had one, and sometimes more than one, previous application. The ratio between first and repeat applications was more or less the same in the case of barring applications alone. If we project this small sample pattern onto the national statistics (which admittedly is a dubious leap), then we would conclude that about 3,000 of the barring applications made in 1993-94 were first-time applications, while the remainder (about 1,500) were repeat applications either from the same year or earlier years. The anecdotal evidence mentioned above would suggest that this is a reasonable broad estimate of the incidence of new barring cases in the year 1993-94.

Success Rate of Barring Applications

A further question about the meaning of the statistics on barring applications arises from the somewhat low rate of success of barring applications. In 1993-94, as Table 2.1 shows, only 45 per cent of barring applications were granted (2,010 out of 4,457). Does this mean that many barring applications are somehow weak or invalid — that while the very fact of applying for a barring order must indicate real unhappiness within a marriage, it may not indicate the presence of a violent or abusive spouse? To answer this question, we need to consider the reasons why a barring application might not be granted. There are three main reasons: the court might refuse the application, it might adjourn the case, or the applicant might not appear in court to pursue the application (in which instance the application is dismissed). In our sample of 132 cases in the DMD Court, 50 involved barring applications. Of these, 27 were granted (54 per cent), 7 were refused (14 per cent), 8 were adjourned (16 per cent) and in 8 cases (16 per cent) the applicant did not appear in court. Though based on a very small sample, these patterns seem broadly consistent with those reported to us by court officials on the basis of their impressions and experience of the system.

We can look at each reason for non-granting in turn to see what it can tell us about the nature of non-granted applications. First, let us look at refusals. From the sketchy details available to us, it appears that in the 7 barring applications in our DMD sample which were refused by the court, the most common allegation against the respondent spouse was alcoholism (5 cases), allied in two cases with drug addiction and in one case with violence. In the two other cases, the principal allegations against the husband were adultery and mental or emotional cruelty. From this it might be reasonable to infer that the typical basis for refusal of the applications was inadequate grounds. The grounds for granting barring orders can be interpreted quite restrictively, such that it may not be sufficient to show that a spouse presents a risk to the safety or welfare of the other spouse ar d/or their children, but that such a risk arises from "serious misconduct" on the offending spouse's part which is "wilful and avoidable" (see above, p. 21). In the absence of actual or threatened violence, alcoholism or even drug addiction on their own may not be interpreted as meeting these conditions, however disruptive and welfare-threatening they may be to the family, and so may be deemed not to warrant the granting of barring orders. Refusals of barring applications, therefore, generally seem to arise where the family involved does show sign of serious dysfunction but not of the specific kind likely to meet the legal criteria for granting a barring order.

In any event, while refusals are an important part of the response by the District Court to barring applications, our limited data suggest that they are relatively uncommon. This in turn may reflect the screening function of District Court clerks and solicitors who would discourage clients from making applications for barring orders if they did not seem to have adequate legal grounds. The more common reasons for non-granting of applications are adjournments on the part of the court and failure to appear on the part of the applicant. Adjournments are often made to allow the respondent spouse the opportunity to amend his ways before the court makes a decision, for example, by seeking treatment for alcoholism or counselling for personality problems. Such deferrals of decisions are often based on the view that while the offending spouse might justifiably be barred, other avenues should be tried before that drastic solution is imposed. Adjournments may also sometimes reflect hesitancy and uncertainty on the part of judges in arriving at decisions. Family conflicts can be complex and bitter and can seem irrational or impossible to adjudicate to court judges, especially given their lack of specialised training either in the law or psychology of family conflict (Law Reform Commission, 1994). The temptation is always present, therefore, to defer decision on a case in the hope that the parties may somehow be able to work out an agreement between themselves.

Non-appearances on the part of applicants are more difficult to interpret since no information is available on why they occur. There are numerous possibilities — reform on the part of the offending spouse, spontaneous departure of the offending spouse from the family home, possibly hastened by the wife's securing of a protection order, weakening of resolve on the part of the applicant which leads her not to pursue the application (perhaps out of fear of her husband or as a consequence of some other form of physical or psychological pressure), uncertainty on the applicant's part as to whether the application will stand up in court, and so on.

Looking at the reasons for non-granting of applications, therefore, there is no indication that the high rate of non-granting reflects a high incidence of unwarranted recourse to barring procedures by spouses. This is so especially in that, more often than not, non-granting means something other than refusal. Adjournment of the case by the court and non-appearance at the hearing by the applicant seem to be the more common forms of non-granting, neither of which necessarily reflects on the seriousness of the underlying difficulties within the family. Even those applications which are refused

often appear to relate to genuine hard cases, though perhaps
not hard enough to fit the terms required for the granting of
barring orders.

In summary, therefore, if we subject the statistics on barring applications to critical scrutiny and sift out the element of
double counting they contain, we are still left with a large and
solid core of genuine barring cases. The size of this core seems
to indicate that a large proportion of marital breakdown cases
arriving before the courts in Ireland are precipitated by violence or abuse on the part of one spouse against either the
other spouse or their children, or indeed both. They also seem
to indicate that this is the single most common form of marital
breakdown which appears before the family courts in Ireland.

Maintenance Applications

Maintenance applications in the District Court are made
mainly under the Family Law (Maintenance of Children and
Spouses) Act, 1976. They may also be made under the Maintenance Orders Act, 1974, which allows for reciprocal enforcement of maintenance orders between Ireland and the United
Kingdom. The District Court has the power to award maintenance up to a maximum of £200 per week for a spouse and £60
a week for a child. Applications for higher amounts must be
made to the Circuit Court.

In the year 1993-94, 2,943 maintenance applications were
made in the District Court, of which 2,241 (76 per cent) were
granted. Ninety-seven per cent of maintenance applications
were made under the 1976 Act, the remainder under the 1974
Act. A certain portion of maintenance applications arise because the Department of Social Welfare requires applicants for
Deserted Wives Benefit and Lone Parents Allowance to show
that they have made efforts to obtain maintenance from their
spouses or partners. Many of the applications for maintenance
in the District Court which result from this requirement have
a *pro forma* character and are likely to result either in refusals
of the application (usually on the grounds that the respondent
has no means to pay maintenance) or in awards of maintenance that have no prospect of being fulfilled.

Most maintenance applications arise between married partners and represent a dimension of marital separation, loosely defined. Some, however, arise in circumstances other than marital separation in the usual sense. A certain proportion are made in conjunction with barring applications and could be considered a dimension of protection procedures for women and children rather than of separation in the usual sense. Clients applying for barring orders who are financially dependent on their spouses are often advised to include a maintenance application with the barring application on the grounds that the question of maintenance would be likely to arise anyway in the event that the barring application is granted (cf. Duncan and Scully, 1990, p. 100). We have no national statistical evidence on the extent to which barring and maintenance applications are submitted jointly in this way, but in our DMD Court sample, it occurred among nine of the 48 maintenance cases in the sample (that is, about 20 per cent).

The second common circumstance in which maintenance applications arise outside of "normal" marital separation is that where non-married partners are involved. In the DMD Court sample, a quarter of maintenance applications were made by unmarried mothers against the fathers of their child (unmarried mothers can claim maintenance from the father only for their children, not for themselves). Some of these might be quasi-separation cases, in that the partners may have cohabited for a time and then separated, whereas in others, the partners may never have lived together so that the question of separation would not arise. We have no information on the incidence of these kinds of circumstances among non-married partners involved in maintenance cases.

In the DMD Court sample, therefore, just over half of the maintenance cases arose in the context of what we might call "pure" marital separation (i.e. involving wives and husbands where barring proceedings were not being invoked). The balance was made up of maintenance cases which were tied in with barring applications (one-fifth of the total) and maintenance cases between non-married partners (one quarter of the total).

Guardianship Applications

Applications for guardianship in the District Court are so labelled in that they arise under the Guardianship of Infants Act, 1964. The label is misleading in that it includes applications for access and custody as well as for guardianship. Section 11 of the 1964 Act gives the District Court jurisdiction over access and custody matters — it empowers the court "to give such directions as it thinks proper regarding the custody of the infant and the right of access to the infant of his father or mother" (see Duncan and Scully, 1990, p. 352). Applications may normally be made only by a guardian of the child, which includes the mother of the child and the father if he is married to the mother. Unmarried fathers do not have automatic rights of guardianship, but they may apply to the court to be appointed guardians under the 1964 Act, as amended by the 1987 Status of Children Act. If appointed as guardian, the unmarried father has the right to apply for custody or access under the 1964 Act in the normal way.

In Table 2.1 above, the data for guardianship include applications for access and custody as well as for guardianship. Together, these applications numbered 3,665 in 1993-94 and form the next largest category of family law business in the District Court after barring applications. A large proportion of these applications arise between separating spouses but, as with maintenance applications, a certain proportion arise in conjunction with barring cases or involve non-married partners. Unlike maintenance cases, a large proportion of guardianship cases are initiated by men. Indeed, guardianship applications in the District Court are the only major family law procedure where the applicant is more likely to be a man than a woman. In the DMD Court sample, 43 cases (one-third of the sample) involved guardianship issues. The applicants were men in 29 (i.e. two-thirds) of these cases and, of these 29 men, 16 (i.e. over half) were unmarried. In addition, two of the guardianship cases were taken by unmarried women. Taking unmarried male and female applicants together, 42 per cent of the guardianship cases in the sample involved unmarried partners.

The most common issue in guardianship cases in the DMD Court sample was access, followed by custody. In nine of the 43 cases, the applicant was an unmarried father seeking to be appointed a guardian of his child and in all but one of these an application for access was made at the same time as the application to be appointed guardian. At the national level, according to Department of Justice data, applications by unmarried fathers seeking to be appointed as guardians of their children accounted for 15 per cent of all guardianship applications in 1993-94. Some such cases may arise among cohabiting couples seeking to strengthen the man's legal relationship with their child or children, and so belong to the realm of family constitution rather than family breakdown. Others undoubtedly originate from unmarried fathers seeking to gain access to children who are normally living with their mother only and are roughly parallel to the types of conflicts found in marital separation.

Guardianship applications are linked with barring applications for much the same reason that maintenance applications are. Questions of custody and access (particularly access) could well arise in the aftermath of a barring order being granted so that it is often advisable to deal with those questions at the same time as the barring application. Guardianship applications may also arise where a barred spouse applies to the court to allow him access to his children. In general, it seems that the combination of barring plus guardianship applications is somewhat less common than the combination of barring plus maintenance applications, though it does occur on a significant scale. One in seven guardianship applications in the DMD Court sample were combined with barring applications, compared to one in five of maintenance applications.

In summary, guardianship proceedings appear to be linked to what we have previously called "pure" marital separation (i.e. cases of husbands and wives who have separated without recourse to barring procedures) somewhat less extensively than are maintenance proceedings. In the DMD sample, the latter occurred between married couples in over half of cases, while something less than half of guardianship proceedings arise between married couples. Guardianship proceedings are quite likely to arise between unmarried partners, and are quite likely to be initiated by unmarried fathers seeking to be appointed as guardians of their children or to obtain access to those children.

Guardianship proceedings are bound up with barring proceedings in a small number of cases, usually where a wife seeks to have the court regulate her barred husband's access to their children.

Estimating the Number and Type of District Court Family Law Cases

Having examined the main categories of family law proceedings appearing before the District Court, we can now return to the question of how many cases underlie the 14,274 family law applications made to the District Court in 1993-94, given that a single case may involve more than one application. We also need to consider the number of new cases within that total and the number which were repeat cases that had made previous appearances before the courts.

In trying to arrive at a count of cases from the count of applications, we can first eliminate the 3,091 applications for protection orders. All of these were made by a sub-set of those who made the 4,457 barring applications and in that sense are double counts with barring applications. By eliminating this obvious element of double counting, the total applications to consider in 1993-94 reduces to 11,183. The degree of double or treble counting of cases within that latter total is not at all obvious, though from what we have seen it is likely to be extensive. In the absence of any better guide, we have to rely on the DMD Court sample to clarify this issue. Within that sample, discounting applications for protection, 70 per cent of the 132 cases were single applications, 22 per cent were double applications, and 8 per cent were treble applications. If this ratio of 70:22:8 between single, double and treble applications were to hold across family law applications in the District Court nationally, it would require about 8,300 cases to produce the 11,183 applications (excluding protection applications) made to the District Court in 1993-94. We will take this total of 8,300 as a rough estimate of the number of separate cases appearing before the District Court in 1993-94.

The DMD Court sample can also give us some guidance on the incidence of repeat cases within the latter total. In collecting data on the DMD sample, we asked the court registrar to indicate whether or not the cases in the sample had made previous applications to the family court. Of the 121 cases for which this information was recorded, 64 per cent (77 cases) had no previous application, 19 per cent (23 cases) had one previous application and the remaining 17 per cent (21 cases) had more than one. Thus, 64 per cent of cases in the sample could be counted as new or first time cases, the remainder as repeats who had made previous applications. If we apply these percentages to our estimate of 8,300 family law cases in the District Court in 1993-94, then we would estimate that about 5,300 of these were new cases.

We should emphasise that the statistical basis for the derivation of this number is uncertain, since it is based on a small sample confined to the Dublin Metropolitan District Court. However, no better basis is available at present, and it is broadly consistent with the impressionistic estimates made to us by court officials and solicitors. It seems reasonable to take it as an indicator of the broad order of magnitude involved, if not a precise estimate. *On that basis, we will take it for the purposes of this study that over 8,000 separate family law cases appeared before the District Court in 1993-94 and over 5,000 of these were new cases.*

We can also indicate in an approximate way the breakdown of these cases between types of proceedings (Table 2.2). In our examination above of statistics on barring applications in the District Court, we estimated that about 3,000 new cases involving barring procedures appeared before the District Court in the same year (along with 1,500 cases that had been before the courts before, either for barring procedures or some other procedure in family law). This would indicate that well over half of the family law caseload in the District Court is centred on barring procedures. This leaves about 2,000 new cases and 1,500 repeat cases which were not centred on barring procedures. These would seem to have been divided between main-

tenance and guardianship procedures in roughly similar proportions, though because of compound cases involving a number of applications, it is difficult to apportion the caseload
across these procedures in any clear-cut way. It is also clear
that a substantial minority of maintenance and guardianship
cases involve non-married partners. In guardianship proceedings especially, non-married partners would appear to account
for something of the order of 40 per cent of the applications.

**Table 2.2: Approximate Size and Composition of Family Law
Caseload in District Court, 1993-94**

Type of Application	New cases	Repeat cases	Total
Protection/barring	3,000	1,500	4,500
Maintenance	1,000	750	1,750
Guardianship	1,000	750	1,750
Total	5,000	3,000	8,000

Judicial Separations

As we turn to judicial separation proceedings, we move from
the District Court to the Circuit Court and come to what is often regarded as the centrepiece of the family law response to
marital breakdown in Ireland. Separation proceedings are
normally composite actions, involving not only separation itself
but also any of a range of ancillary issues such as maintenance, division of family property, custody and access. All of
these issues can be dealt with in the Circuit Court under the
Judicial Separation and Family Law Reform Act, 1989.

The count of judicial separation applications for 1993-94 reported in Table 2.1 above is 2,806, which is a good deal less
than half our estimated total of all family law cases in the District Court (8,300) and only a little more than half the estimated total of new family law cases in the District Court
(5,300).

Of the 2,806 judicial separation applications made in 1993-
94, only 986 (35 per cent) were granted. This low success rate
in judicial separation applications is probably more a function

of the backlog of family cases in the Circuit Court than anything else. Delays of anything from six months to a year are
commonly reported in getting family law cases listed for hearing in the Circuit Court, and even then adjournments are
common as the courts cannot find the time to devote the necessary scrutiny to individual cases. We have no information on
the reasons for non-granting of the judicial separation applications in 1993-94 which were not granted (these numbered
1,766), but it is unlikely that anything more than a minority of
them were refused. The majority probably consist of an accu-
mulated backlog waiting to be dealt with by the court.

As we will refer extensively to judicial separation cases in
later chapters, we will not dwell on them any further here.

Trends over Time

We now take a brief look at the available statistics on trends
in the national family law caseload over time.

Figure 2.1, which deals with barring applications and barring orders for the period 1981-94, shows that barring procedures were already relatively common in the early 1980s. In
1981, for example, there were 2,225 barring applications and
1,188 barring orders were granted. The numbers of applications and orders rose in most, though not all, of the interven-
ing years up to 1994. The numbers for 1983 were low on account of strike action by District Court clerks in that year; and
the numbers for the following year may have been inflated to
some extent by the backlog carried over from 1983. By 1994
the number of applications had just about doubled since 1981,
rising to 4,457, and the number of orders had gone up by 70
per cent to 2,010. The cumulative total of barring orders
granted over the period 1981-94 was 19,444, though as noted
before, the number of families involved was likely to have been
a good deal lower on account of a certain incidence of repeat
applications from the same applicants.

Figure 2.1: Barring Applicants and Barring Orders in the District Court, 1981-94

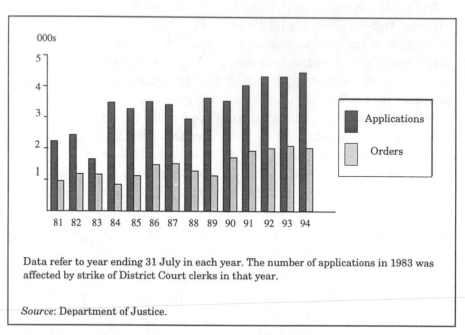

Data refer to year ending 31 July in each year. The number of applications in 1983 was affected by strike of District Court clerks in that year.

Source: Department of Justice.

Maintenance procedures were also numerous in the early 1980s and have generally risen, though somewhat erratically, over the years since then (Figure 2.2). (Again, the data for 1983 should be regarded as anomalous because of the District Court clerks' strike in that year.) The data on maintenance orders granted are unavailable for the mid-1980s, so that the trend picture is not complete. It does appear, however, that the number of orders granted fell in the early 1980s and rose rapidly from the late 1980s onwards — the number of maintenance applications granted in 1994 was 150 per cent higher than in 1988. However, the rise in applications has been less marked, meaning that orders granted as a proportion of applications made has risen in recent years (from 54 per cent in 1988 to 76 per cent in 1994).

Figure 2.2: Applications for Maintenance and Maintenance Orders Granted in District Court, 1981-94

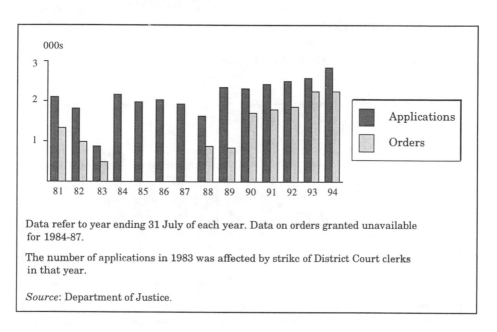

Data refer to year ending 31 July of each year. Data on orders granted unavailable for 1984-87.

The number of applications in 1983 was affected by strike of District Court clerks in that year.

Source: Department of Justice.

Data on applications for guardianship in the District Court go back only to 1987 and no data are available on orders granted. The number of applications has risen more than three-fold over that period, going from 1,160 in 1987 to 3,665 in 1994 (Figure 2.3). This is a much sharper rate of increase than occurred either with barring or maintenance applications. Part of the explanation for the increase lies with the Status of Children Act 1987, which amended the Guardianship of Children Act of 1964 so as to increase the rights of unmarried fathers with regard to guardianship and custody of their children. It is likely also, however, that apart from any changes in the law, from the late 1980s onwards unmarried fathers began to show an increasing interest in exercising such rights as they already had, particularly the right of access which had long been in place under the 1964 Act but which hitherto had been little used. Unmarried mothers may also have cause to make applications concerning access and custody, especially where they wish the court to regulate informal arrangements which have emerged with the fathers of their children, or to adjudicate on conflicts on these questions. As we saw earlier, something less than half of the guardianship cases in the DMD Court sample involved unmarried partners.

Figure 2.3: Applications for Guardianship in the District Court, 1987-94

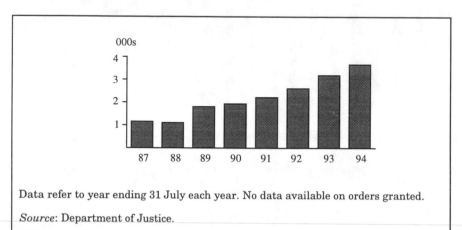

Data refer to year ending 31 July each year. No data available on orders granted.

Source: Department of Justice.

Until the Judicial Separation and Family Law Reform Act, 1989 came into force, the Circuit Court was empowered to grant judicial separation in the form of decrees of divorce *a mensa et thora* under the Matrimonial Causes Act, 1870 and the Courts Act, 1981. During the 1980s, separation proceedings under this arrangement were relatively few (Figure 2.4). In 1982, for example, there were only five applications and three orders granted, while in 1988 there were 217 applications and 92 orders granted. Since the 1989 Act came into force, the numbers of applications have increased sharply, particularly up to 1993. In that year, there were 2,781 applications and 1,015 orders were granted. Some levelling off is apparent in 1994. While the total number of applications had risen slightly to 2,081, the number of orders granted had fallen slightly to 986. This levelling off could indicate a levelling off in the underlying incidence of marital breakdown. It is more likely, however, that it is due the reaching of peak capacity in the Circuit Court so that the system is unable to cope with any increase in numbers.

Figure 2.4: Applications and Orders for Divorce *a Mensa et Thora*, 1982-89, and for Judicial Separation, 1990-94

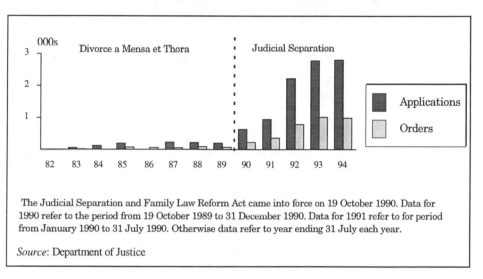

The Judicial Separation and Family Law Reform Act came into force on 19 October 1990. Data for 1990 refer to the period from 19 October 1989 to 31 December 1990. Data for 1991 refer to for period from January 1990 to 31 July 1990. Otherwise data refer to year ending 31 July each year.

Source: Department of Justice

Even with the growth in the numbers of judicial separation cases in the 1990s, the level reached by 1993 and 1994 is still relatively low, at least by comparison with volume of family law business in the District Court. This reflects the low base of judicial separation cases in the Circuit Court up to the late 1980s from which the recent growth began. The lowness in the incidence of judicial separation is especially evident if we look at orders granted rather than applications, since the former is still only at around 1,000 in 1993-94. We should recall that in the same year, barring orders alone granted in the District Court numbered 2,241.

Distribution by County

Tables 2.3 and 2.4, which are appended to this chapter, indicate the distribution by county of family law applications in the District Court and Circuit Court in 1993-94. Data on the county by county distribution of the married population are also included in Table 2.4 to indicate the distribution of the population at risk of marital separation.

Certain puzzling patterns emerge from the county distributions. One is the odd position of Dublin. It is heavily over-represented in District Court applications — it accounts for half the national total, though it accounts for only 28 per cent of the population of married persons. On the other hand, Dublin is heavily *under-represented* in judicial separation applications in the Circuit Court — here it accounts for only 14 per cent of the applications made. We can only speculate as to why Dublin stands out in these contradictory directions. It may be that the backlog effect in the Circuit Court is weaker in Dublin than in the rest of the country — other areas may be now catching up with Dublin and lodging separation applications at a greater rate, even though the Circuit Court in those areas may not be as well geared up to process those applications as it is in Dublin. Thus, for example, Cork and Galway have more applications for judicial separation than Dublin but much lower numbers of applications granted.

These regional patterns in judicial separation, however, do not help us account for the huge volume of family law business in the District Court in Dublin. Cork has less than a quarter the number of District Court applications in Dublin, and Galway has less than one-eleventh the Dublin total. The prominence of Dublin in the District Court statistics may be a function of the level and kind of family breakdown which occurs in Dublin or it may be a function of the court system in some way —the District Court in Dublin has better facilities and so is more accessible to clients than it is in other parts of the country.

It is also worth noting from Table 2.4 that the rate of granting of applications for judicial separation in the Circuit Court varies enormously by county. For the state as a whole, 35 per cent of applications were granted. At the extreme above this average, applications granted amounted to 84 per cent of applications made in Dublin, and in certain smaller circuits, such as Wexford, Kilkenny, Clare and Sligo, the granting rate was even higher (granting rates of 100 per cent or over in Wexford, Kilkenny and Clare reflect a carry-over of applications from the previous year). At the other extreme, only 11 per cent of applications were granted in Tipperary, 12 per cent in Kildare and 13 per cent in Galway. The only factor we can adduce to explain these variations is the backlog of cases. While waiting times and backlogs for family law hearings in the Circuit Court are widespread in practically all circuits, they may be worse in some than in others and may lead to an extreme degree of build-up of cases in the worst-affected circuits.

Conclusion

This chapter has reviewed Department of Justice statistics on court proceedings in family law in Ireland, supplemented by a certain amount of information drawn from our DMD Court sample. The objective has been to get an initial impression of the type and frequency of family law cases appearing before the courts in Ireland.

Two main conclusions emerge from the chapter. The first is that the District Court rather than the Circuit Court is the main locus of family law practice in the court system in Ireland. We estimate roughly that in excess of 8,000 family law cases appeared before the District Court in 1993-94, of which more than 5,000 were new cases and the remainder were repeats which had been before the courts previously. These estimates are approximate but they seem sufficiently reliable to indicate the orders of magnitude involved. The Circuit Court received 2,806 applications for judicial separation in 1993-94 (judicial separation accounts for the vast majority of family law business in the Circuit Court). It thus would appear that the number of all family law cases in the Circuit Court in 1993-94 was a good deal less than half the number of all District Court cases, while the number of new family law cases in the Circuit Court was probably just over half the number of new cases in the District Court. In short, in terms of numbers of cases dealt with in the courts, the District Court is roughly twice as important as the Circuit Court in the Irish family law system.

The second major conclusion of the chapter is that family law as operated through the courts in Ireland has two major functions. The first, and marginally dominant, of these is the protection function — the protection of wives and children from violence on the part of husbands/fathers. It is expressed principally through protection and barring proceedings in the District Court. Maintenance and custody/access proceedings are sometimes added to barring proceedings in order to deal with the consequences of barring orders being granted, but nevertheless, the central issue in this area of family law is protection of family members against domestic violence, mainly by husbands/fathers.

The second major function of the court system in family law is marital separation in the more usual sense. This function is exercised partly in the Circuit Court under the Judicial Separation and Family Law Reform Act, 1989, and partly in the District Court under a range of statutes which provide piecemeal, partial coverage of issues arising out of marital separation. It is a more diffuse function than the protection function in that it is spread over the two court levels and over a range of statutes, but it has a constant underlying concern with regulation of the consequences of marital breakdown where violence has not been adduced as the key issue for the courts to deal with.

In certain senses, the distinction between the protection and separation functions is far from absolute. Protection may often amount to separation under another name, in that the wife's intention may be to effect a permanent parting of the ways from her husband, and domestic violence may lie in the background to many separation cases in which the protection function is not directly invoked. However, this blurring of the boundaries between the protection and separation functions occurs beyond or behind the surface processing of court cases. We will further consider the overlaps involved in Chapter Seven below, but here will proceed on the basis that the distinction between the protection and separation functions corresponds to procedural practice and has sufficient meaning to warrant considerable attention.

Along with these two major functions, there is an additional more marginal element in court proceedings in family law. This consists of proceedings involving non-married partners.

This element is marginal partly in a statistical sense, in that the cases which comprise it are much fewer than those arising under the two main functions, and partly in a legal sense, in that the range of proceedings which non-married partners can invoke is much narrower than that available to married partners. These proceedings are largely confined to two areas — maintenance proceedings under the Family Law (Maintenance of Spouses and Children) Act, 1976 and guardianship proceedings under the Guardianship of Infants Act, 1964, as amended by the 1987 Status of Children Act. Furthermore, these proceedings take place almost exclusively in the District Court. Barring procedures cannot be invoked by non-married partners and neither can the comprehensive provisions of the Judicial Separation and Family Law Reform Act, 1989. In many cases, non-marital litigation could be considered a rough parallel to marital litigation in the District Court — for example, an unmarried mother seeking maintenance for her child from the man with whom she had lived for a period of years might be in a broadly similar position to a wife taking a maintenance case against a husband. In other cases, however, non-marital litigation reflects the distinctive circumstances of unmarried partners, especially where unmarried fathers seek to be appointed guardians of their children.

In broad terms, therefore, the family law system as expressed through the courts in Ireland can be considered a two function system (protection and marital separation) that operates mainly on two levels (the District Court and the Circuit Court). These two dualisms seem to parallel each other to a great extent — the protection function is heavily concentrated in the District Court while the Circuit Court is overwhelmingly concerned with marital separation. However, the parallel is far from complete since the separation function is also a major concern of the District Court. Litigation between non-marital partners adds a smaller function to the system which is integrated mainly into the District Court level. In the following chapters, we will explore the nature of these dualisms further and examine how they relate to each other and to further aspects of the family law system.

Table 2.3: District Court Family Law Applications by County*
and District Court Office, 1993-94

County	Office	Type of Application				Total	
		Maintenance	Guardianship	Barring	Protection	Number	%
Carlow	Carlow	24	29	22	16	91	0.6
Dublin	Dublin	1,079	1,786	2,325	1,798	6,988	49.4
Kildare	Naas	83	70	142	88	383	2.7
Kilkenny	Kilkenny	50	22	48	19	139	1.0
Laois	Portlaoise	42	50	51	29	172	1.2
Longford	Longford	24	16	40	20	100	0.7
Louth	Drogheda	98	144	68	43	353	4.2
	Dundalk	45	95	55	52	247	
Meath	Trim	36	64	57	60	217	1.5
Offaly	Tullamore	29	12	36	25	102	0.7
Westmeath	Athlone	23	11	34	24	92	1.6
	Mullingar	33	28	45	27	133	
Wexford	Gorey	31	16	17	6	70	2.1
	Wexford	70	50	57	47	224	
Wicklow	Bray	104	86	103	71	364	2.6
Clare	Ennis	76	47	85	66	274	1.9
Cork	Bandon	30	27	41	37	135	
	Cork	345	299	280	211	1135	
	Fermoy	25	18	19	18	80	11
	Mallow	20	24	31	19	94	
	Yougal	21	27	38	28	114	
Kerry	Killarney	32	9	35	1	77	
	Listowel	15	0	27	14	56	2.2
	Tralee	40	30	66	41	177	
Limerick	Limerick	90	121	170	96	477	3.3
Tipperary	Clonmel	67	21	60	39	187	
	Nenagh	16	22	18	8	64	2.2
	Thurles	23	23	22	0	68	
Waterford	Waterford	47	55	38	22	162	1.1

Table 2.3: District Court Family Law Applications by County* and District Court Office, 1993-94 (continued)

County	Office	Type of Application				Total	
		Maintenance	Guardianship	Barring	Protection	Number	%
Galway	Ballinasloe	8	15	30	4	57	
	Derrynea	2	6	3	0	11	
	Galway	77	162	77	54	370	3.8
	Loughrea	11	25	19	4	59	
	Tuam	11	10	9	5	35	
Leitrim	Carrick-on-Shannon	11	12	12	0	35	0.3
Mayo	Ballina	29	16	15	10	70	0.9
	Castlebar	19	17	17	7	60	
Roscommon	Roscommon	10	4	11	0	25	0.2
Sligo	Sligo	28	23	45	28	124	0.9
Cavan	Cavan	32	61	29	8	130	0.9
Donegal	Donegal	25	23	26	13	87	1.9
	Letterkenny	22	58	82	21	183	
Monaghan	Monaghan	40	31	52	12	135	1.0
State		**2,943**	**3,665**	**4,457**	**3,091**	**14,156**	**100**

* Data are compiled by District Court Office. The catchment areas of District Court Offices do not always correspond to county boundaries, so that the tabulation of the data by county should be regarded as approximate.

Source: Department of Justice.

Table 2.4: Applications for Judicial Separation in Circuit Court by County, 1993-94

County	Applications Made		Applications Granted		Distribution of Married Population (1991) %
	Number	%	Number	As % of applications made	
Carlow	23	0.8	6	26.1	1.2
Dublin	395	14.1	327	83.8	28.4
Kildare	167	6	20	12.1	3.6
Kilkenny	14	0.5	14	100	2.1
Laois	45	1.6	12	26.7	1.5
Longford	6	0.2	4	66.7	0.9
Louth	32	1.1	32	100	2.6
Meath	32	1.1	23	71.9	3.1
Offaly	61	2.2	15	24.6	1.7
Westmeath	20	0.7	20	100	1.8
Wexford	14	0.5	19	135.7	3
Wicklow	194	6.9	40	20.6	2.9
Clare	14	0.5	14	100	2.7
Cork	547	19.5	134	24.5	11.8
Kerry	59	2.1	17	28.8	3.5
Limerick	223	8	37	16.6	4.6
Tipperary	101	3.6	11	10.9	3.8
Waterford	30	1.1	12	40	2.6
Galway	556	19.8	71	12.8	4.9
Leitrim	22	0.8	9	40.9	0.7
Mayo	30	1.1	12	40	3.2
Roscommon	20	0.7	21	105	1.5
Sligo	35	1.3	33	94.3	1.5
Cavan	17	0.6	13	76.5	1.5
Donegal	50	1.8	37	74	3.6
Monaghan	99	3.5	36	36.4	1.4
State	**2,806**	**100**	**989**	**35.3**	**100**

Applications granted may exceed applications made since applications may be carried over from previous year. Counties are grouped by province.

Sources: Department of Justice; Census of Population, 1991.

CHAPTER 3

SOCIAL PROFILE OF SAMPLE CASES

In this chapter we describe the family and social characteristics of those who make use of the family law system. The information source used is the solicitors' case file sample. This means that the focus is on those family law cases where solicitors were involved. In consequence, legally unrepresented cases, which, as we saw in Chapter One make up a large proportion of the District Court caseload, are largely missing from the social profile. While we attempted to collect information on the social characteristics of legally unrepresented cases from the DMD Court sample, the information obtained lacked the detail and completeness necessary for useful analysis. The present chapter, therefore, cannot offer insight into this large and important segment of the family law caseload.

In referring to the legally represented cases which are the focus of the chapter, we draw a major distinction between those who are represented by private solicitors and those represented by solicitors of the Legal Aid Board. This is so partly on technical grounds, in that the two types of cases were sampled separately and therefore cannot be readily aggregated into a single sample (see Appendix I). But the distinction is also relevant to the substance of the present chapter, in that we would expect major social differences between private and legal aid clients. Civil legal aid is granted to clients on the basis of means, so that the economic circumstances of legal aid recipients can be expected to be significantly poorer than those of private clients (see Appendix III).

We begin with an account of the personal and family circumstances of clients in the solicitors' case file sample — their age, type and duration of relationship with the other party, and number of dependent children. We then consider the socio-economic circumstances of clients and their partners — their income sources, employment status and social class position.

Personal and Family Characteristics

Type of Relationship

Table 3.1 shows that over 90 per cent of the solicitor's clients included in our study are or had been married to the other party involved in the case. The remainder were unmarried. While the sub-sample of unmarried partners is too small to allow for further analysis, it appears that non-cohabiting relationships or cohabitation of less than one year were as common as longer-term cohabitation. Legal aid clients were somewhat more likely to be unmarried (15 per cent) than private clients (6 per cent).

Table 3.1: Nature of Client's Relationship with the Principal Other Party in the Case by Type of Legal Representation (in %)

Nature of Relationship	Type of Legal Representation		
	Private	Legal Aid	All
Marriage	94	85	91
Cohabiting less than 1 year	1	2	5
Cohabiting 1 year or more	4	7	1
Non-cohabiting relationship	1	5	3
Other	-	1	-
Total	100	100	100
(N)	(355)	(151)	(506)

The age-profile of clients is presented in Table 3.2. The age-range from the mid-30s to the late 40s accounts for well over half the sample. One-third are aged 40-49 and a further one-fifth are aged 35-39. Very few are aged under 25 and of these over half are unmarried. At the other extreme, one-fifth of the clients are aged over 50 and of these practically all are married. Unmarried clients in the sample, in fact, are mainly found among those still in their 20s. As one would expect also, the younger the unmarried person, the less likely that the relationship in which he or she was involved was a long-term co-habitation. The age-profiles of the sample differed little between private and legal aid cases, except that those aged 50 and over are more prevalent among private cases.

Table 3.2: Age of Clients by Type of Legal Representation (in %)

Age	Type of Legal Representation		
	Private	*Legal Aid*	*All*
Less than 25 years	4	4	4
25-34 years	21	29	24
35-39 years	20	21	20
40-49 years	35	35	35
50+ years	20	11	17
Total	100	100	100
(N)	(354)	(151)	(505)

The age-profile of married clients in the sample differed from that of the total married population mainly in that married people aged 50 and over are heavily under-represented in the sample, while those aged 35-49 are over-represented. This would suggest that the late 30s and 40s are the high risk ages for marital breakdown in Ireland — or at least for the type of marital breakdown which results in family law cases.

Duration of Relationship

Turning to the duration of the clients' relationship, Table 3.3 indicates that the general pattern is towards longer rather than shorter durations. About two-thirds of the sample have relationship durations of 11 years or more, and over a quarter have durations of 21 years or more. If one removed the unmarried from the picture, the incidence of longer durations would rise somewhat further. At the same time, there is a significant minority whose relationships are quite short: 8 per cent of private clients and 9 per cent of legal aid clients had relationship durations of three years or less.

Table 3.3: Duration of Relationship by Type of Legal Representation (in %)

	Type of Legal Representation		
	Private	Legal Aid	All
Less than 1 year	3	1	3
1-3 years	5	8	6
4-5 years	7	9	7
6-10 years	16	18	17
11-15 years	23	16	21
16-20 years	19	21	19
21+ years	27	27	27
Total	100	100	100
(N)	(354)	(142)	(496)

Number of Children

The vast majority of family law clients had children (83 per cent). For some of these, the children were grown up (aged over 18), so that the proportion with what we could consider as dependent children was 79 per cent (Table 3.4). Typically, over half (54 per cent) of these couples had either one or two children. There were some differences between private and legal aid clients in number of dependent children: private clients were slightly more likely to have no dependent children (23 per cent) than legal aid clients (18 per cent), while legal aid clients were more likely to have three or more dependent children (32 per cent) than private clients (22 per cent).

Socio-Economic Circumstances

Information collected from solicitors on the socio-economic circumstances of clients related to clients' housing tenure, employment status and occupation, principal income source and amount of net weekly income. The information on occupation was also used to classify clients by social class. No information was gathered on clients' education, on the grounds that solicitors usually would not have that information.

Table 3.4: Number of Dependent Children by Type of Legal Representation (in %)

	Type of Legal Representation		
	Private	*Legal Aid*	*All*
No children	23	18	21
1 child	29	25	28
2 children	26	25	26
3 children	14	19	15
4 children	5	7	6
5 or more children	3	6	4
Total	100	100	100
(N)	(355)	(151)	(506)

Before looking at this information, we should recall its second-hand nature — it was obtained from solicitors rather than from clients themselves or their partners. Questions about jobs, income and housing are usually of central interest in family law cases and solicitors usually have considerable information on these issues, not only about their clients but also about the spouse or partner on the other side. This is not to say, however, that the information is always accurate. Neither clients nor their spouses/partners might want to tell the full story about their jobs, incomes and housing circumstances. They would often tend, rather, to overstate how badly off they were, either to justify a claim for maintenance or property transfer from the other side or to show why they could not meet such a claim if it were being made against them. Rarely would there be a contrary tendency for either side in a family law case to overstate their level of material well-being. In looking at the information which follows, therefore, we should keep in made the possible tendency to overstate the incidence of unemployment and other forms of bad fortune which might lie behind it.

Housing Tenure

The majority of clients were living in owner-occupied housing (76 per cent), usually with a mortgage rather than with outright ownership (Table 3.5). However, there were clear differences on this count between private and legal aid clients. The proportion of private clients living in owner-occupied housing was almost twice that of legal aid clients (88 per cent and 47 per cent respectively). Conversely, legal aid clients were five times more likely to be living in local authority housing than private clients. Similarly, the remaining categories of "private rented" and "no family home" are more than three times more likely to occur among legal aid clients.

Table 3.5: Housing Tenure by Type of Legal Representation (in %)

| | Type of Legal Representation | | |
	Private	Legal Aid	All
Owned with mortgage	69	38	60
Owned no mortgage	19	9	16
Private rented	3	11	6
Local authority	5	26	11
No family home	3	11	5
Other	1	5	2
Total	100	100	100
(N)	(355)	(151)	(506)

In the national population, according to the 1991 Census of Population, 80 per cent of non-institutional households live in owner-occupied housing. Local Authority housing and private rented accommodation account for ten and eight per cent respectively, while the remaining two per cent of households are in rent-free housing. Taking these figures as a reference, the sample patterns shown in Table 3.5 suggest that owner-occupied housing is slightly over-represented among private clients while Local Authority and private renting accommodation is slightly under-represented. Among legal aid clients, the divergence from national patterns is much sharper: less than half are owner-occupiers, while over a quarter (almost three times the national average) are in Local Authority accommodation. Private clients, therefore, are heavily concentrated in the more privileged form of housing tenure. Legal aid clients are more dispersed over tenure types, with large minorities in less privileged forms.

Employment Status

The difference in social profile between private and legal aid clients emerges most clearly when we look at employment status. Table 3.6 draws on information about clients and their spouses/partners to show the employment status of those on both sides of family law cases in the solicitors' case-file sample. Among men, 79 per cent of those connected with private cases are at work, compared to 42 per cent of those connected to legal aid cases, while the proportion unemployed is 14 per cent in private cases and 50 per cent among legal aid cases. Among women, 60 per cent of those connected to private cases are at work compared to 24 per cent among legal aid cases. Among women in private cases, if we add the 9 per cent who are unemployed to the 60 per cent at work, we get a labour force participation rate of 69 per cent. This is well over double the labour force participation rate for all married and separated women aged 35-54 in the national population, which was 30 per cent in 1992 (Labour Force Survey, 1992, Table 12b). The labour force participation rate for women in legal aid cases is also reasonably high at 46 per cent, but almost half of these are unemployed (22 per cent) and of those who are at work half are employed part-time rather than full-time. As a result, labour force attachment among women in legal aid cases is quite weak.

Table 3.7 utilises the same employment data as Table 3.6 but presents it according to the employment status of couples rather than of men and women separately. Two-job couples are the modal type among private cases (47 per cent), while they account for only 10 per cent of legal aid cases. At the other extreme, couples where neither partner has a job accounts for 39 per cent of legal aid cases compared to 5 per cent private cases. The traditional standard family type where the man is at work and the woman in home duties is in a minority of about one-fifth in both private and legal aid cases. Even if we add in the substantial proportion of women in the home who are counted as unemployed rather than in home duties, the total of male breadwinners combined with stay-at-home wife is relatively small.

Table 3.6: Employment Status of Partners* by Type of Legal Representation of Client (in %)

Employment Status	Private		Legal Aid		All	
	Male	Female	Male	Female	Male	Female
At work	79	60	42	24	67	49
Unemployed	14	9	50	22	25	13
Home duties	—	28	2	46	1	33
Other	7	4	6	8	7	5
Total	100	100	100	100	100	100
(N)	(341)	(346)	(145)	(147)	(486)	(493)

* Based on employment status data for clients and their spouses/partners.

Table 3.7: Employment Status of Couples by Type of Legal Representation of Client (in %)

	Private	Legal Aid	All
One or Both Partners in Paid Job:	91	56	80
Both in Paid Jobs	47	10	35
Man in Paid Job; Woman Home Duties	22	17	21
Man in Paid Job; Woman Unemployed	9	16	11
Woman in Paid Job; Man Unemployed	13	13	13
Neither Partner in Paid Job:	5	39	16
Both Unemployed	2	14	6
Man Unemployed, Woman Home Duties	3	25	10
Other	4	5	4
Total	100	100	100
	(332)	(141)	(476)

Principal Source of Income

Employment status by itself does not tell us from what source spouses or partners derive their main income. For example, a woman in home duties may derive her income mainly from her husband (by way of maintenance, for example) or from social welfare. Table 3.8 deals with the question of principal income source, concentrating this time on clients rather than on clients and partners together. The proportion of women who derive their main income from paid work in this table is slightly lower than the proportion at work in Table 3.6, suggesting that for some women with jobs their paid work provides only a secondary income source. Social welfare dependence is very high among legal aid clients (over 80 per cent in the case of men, over 60 per cent in the case of women), while it accounts for a minority, albeit a significant one (almost one-fifth), among private cases. The level of women's dependence on maintenance from their husbands is quite low — 23 per cent for private clients, 10 per cent for legal aid clients.

Table 3.8: Principal Source of Income by Type of Legal Representation by Sex (in %)

Principal Source of Income	Private		Legal Aid		All	
	Male	Female	Male	Female	Male	Female
Own Paid Work	80	50	14	20	65	40
Social Welfare	18	17	86	63	33	33
Support from Co-Residing Spouse	—	9	—	8	—	8
Maintenance	1	23	—	10	1	18
Other	1	1	—	—	1	1
Total	100	100	100	100	100	100
(N)	(154)	(201)	(44)	(107)	(201)	(309)

Income

The income data collected from solicitors' case-files was relatively crude and, as already mentioned, may be subject to considerable under-statement, yet is worth looking at briefly (Table 3.9). Almost a third of legal aid clients are reported to have an income of £60 per week or less, while only a small minority have incomes above £150 per week. Over half of private clients have incomes above £150 per week, and over a quarter are above £250 per week.

Social Class

Information was collected on the occupations of both male and female partners and later categorised into the six point social class scale used in the 1986 Census of Population (see Table 3.10).

Table 3.9: Clients' Net Weekly Income by Type of Legal Representation (in %)

	Type of Legal Representation		
	Private	*Legal Aid*	*All*
< £60	16	31	21
£61 - £150	33	57	40
£151 - £250	24	9	19
£251 - £500	21	3	16
£501+	6	—	4
Total	100	100	100
(N)	(355)	(151)	(506)

Table 3.10: Clients' Social Class by Type of Legal Representation (in %)

Social class		*Type of Legal Representation*			*Population Distribution for All Married Persons (1986 Census)*
		Private	*Legal Aid*	*All*	
I.	Higher professional/ farmers 200 acres	12	2	9	10
II.	Lower professional/ farmers 100-200 acres	21	9	18	14
III.	Other non-manual/ farmers 50-99 acres	34	52	39	18
IV.	Skilled manual/ farmers 30-49 acres	12	11	11	23
V.	Semi-skilled manual/ farmers < 36 acres	8	12	9	15
VI.	Unskilled manual	13	15	14	10
	Total	100	100	100	100
	(N)	(342)	(151)	(493)	

Social class patterns among private and legal aid clients show quite strikingly that the patterns of economic advantage and disadvantage which we have just found to distinguish those two groupings are *not* strongly related to social class. This is so firstly in that the working classes generally (skilled, semi-skilled and unskilled), along with small farmers, are under-represented to a certain extent in the sample (social classes IV, V and VI). More notably, there is no real difference between private and legal aid clients on this issue — the working classes are represented (or rather, under-represented) to a broadly similar degree in both groups. Legal aid, therefore, is not the preserve of the working classes. Rather, the largest proportions of both private and legal aid clients are from social class III (lower non-manual workers and medium farmers). This class is especially dominant among legal aid clients, where it accounts for half of the total. Thus, according to this evidence, to the extent that legal aid is linked with any par-ticular social class, it is with the lower middle class rather than the working classes — though this class is also likely to make heavy use of private solicitors. The professional classes are somewhat over-represented among private clients and are under-represented among legal aid clients. However, some le-gal aid clients are from the professional classes, particularly the lower professions (social class II). This emphasises again the weak linkages between social class and reliance on legal aid.

Given the over-representation of social class III among both private and legal aid clients, it may be worth noting the occu-pations which dominate in this social class grouping in the sample. Just under 40 per cent are farmers or farmers' wives, and indeed virtually *all* of the farmers and farmers' wives in the sample fall into this group. Nationally, according to 1986 Census data, farmers in social class III account for 35 per cent of all farmers. Farmers account for a greater proportion of le-gal aid clients in social class III than private clients — 46 and 31 per cent respectively. Other common occupations in this social class in the sample include clerical workers (14 per cent), typists (6 per cent), bookkeepers (5 per cent) and com-mercial travellers (4 per cent), along with barbers, watchmen, foremen and chefs. Women in home duties were assigned a class position on the basis of their spouse's occupation. This group constitute 20 per cent of social class III. They tend to be over-represented among legal aid clients and under-represented among private clients.

Conclusion

This chapter has described the family and social characteristics of solicitors' family law clients. It first outlined their personal and family characteristics. Solicitors' family law clients for the most part are married, though with a minority of young unmarried people who mainly have had relatively short relationships with their partners. The largest proportions of clients are in the age-range 35-49, though with substantial minorities above and below that range. Among those who were married, most had been in marriages of reasonably long duration — usually ten years or more. Eight out of ten clients have dependent children, and legal aid clients have somewhat larger numbers of children than private clients.

When we turn to the socio-economic characteristics of solicitors' clients, we find relatively high levels of economic disadvantage. We also find that the type of legal representation used by clients is quite strongly related to economic advantage and disadvantage, particularly in connection with employment status and social welfare dependence, but also to some extent in connection with housing tenure. Legal aid cases are associated with high levels of unemployment, especially among the male partners, and high levels of social welfare dependence. They are also less likely to live in owner-occupied housing than the population average. Private cases have a high incidence of two-earner couples and a lower incidence of social welfare dependence, though some unemployment and social welfare dependence does exist in this category. They are somewhat more likely than the national average to live in owner-occupied housing.

We also find, however, that type of legal representation is not linked to social class in the way one might expect — legal aid is more a lower middle class than a working class resource and most social classes, including the working class, straddle the boundary between private and legal aid representation quite extensively. Thus, the unemployed and the welfare de-

pendent who make up such a large proportion of legal aid clientele in family law are not disproportionately drawn from the
working classes. They are more likely to come from the lower
non-manual and medium farming class — and in particular to
be made up of women from this social class. Clients from the
professional classes in general tend to have stronger labour
market positions, but a minority of them too are unemployed
or welfare dependent.

We should recall here that legally unrepresented family law
cases arising in the District Court are missing from the present account of the social circumstances of family law clients.
We do not have the data to identify the economic characteristics or social class composition of such clients. It is possible
that the working classes, which, as we have seen in this chapter, are under-represented somewhat among legally represented family law cases, can be found in greater numbers
among legally unrepresented cases in the District Court, or
even perhaps among those informal separations which make
no contact whatever with family law. This, however, is a question which we cannot answer in the present study.

The patterns identified in this chapter also raise larger
questions about the relationship between economic disadvantage and marital breakdown. The cross-class distribution of
unemployment and social welfare dependence which we have
found in the solicitors' case-file sample may indicate that those
who fall into financial difficulties or experience unemployment
in any social class may be especially prone to marital problems. It may suggest, in other words, that economic stress is
likely to cause marital stress, no matter what social class it
arises in. On the other hand, economic stress may equally be
the consequence rather than the cause of marital problems.
For spouses generally, and wives in particular, marital breakdown may make it difficult to find or hold a job, or may be associated with other problems (such as lack of maintenance
from husbands or lack of child-care services) which drive
households to social welfare dependence. It is well known that
marital breakdown causes major disruption to the economic
circumstances of households, and such disruption may well be
no respector of social class boundaries. Again, however, the

precise relationship between economic strain and marital breakdown is something we cannot investigate properly here.

CHAPTER 4

LEGAL PROFILE OF SAMPLE CASES

In this chapter we turn to a description of the legal features of the family law cases. As in the previous chapter, the information is drawn from the solicitors' case-file sample. We should recall the nature of this information source: it covers only those family law cases in which solicitors have become involved and therefore does not include family law cases which were taken to court without legal representation. As we saw in Chapters One and Two above, legally unrepresented cases are common in the District Court and may comprise something of the order of half of family law cases at that court level. The coverage of family law cases in the present chapter, therefore, is biased towards the Circuit Court and thus towards legal separation proceedings. In other words, it is biased towards what we have earlier referred to as the second function of the family law system in Ireland (that is, separation proceedings rather than barring/protection proceedings). We will return to the implications of this bias later in the report, but for the present will concentrate on the legally represented segment of the family law case load from which our sample is drawn.

In gathering information for a legal profile of the sample cases, it was often quite difficult to reduce the detail of individual cases to a manageable set of categories. This reflects the complex, long drawn out nature of many family law cases. The course of such cases rarely runs smooth. Not only can the issues be complex or difficult at any given time, they can also change in the course of the case, sometime quite rapidly. This is so not only because the circumstances of the partners can change, but also because they will often shift negotiating position, raise new issues or drop old ones in order to maximise tactical advantage. Furthermore, while a range of issues might be included in negotiations, they are unlikely to be equally central. The partners might be in complete agreement about some issues, or think them unimportant, and might be sharply at odds about others. What starts out as a marginal issue might become central because they cannot agree on it. Alternatively, a key issue might be settled early in the case and thus cease to be central for the remainder of the negotiations. The fictional sample case outlined in Box 4.1 illustrates some of the things which can happen, though by the standards of family law cases this would not be a particularly complex example.

The data presented in this chapter present a simplified version of this complexity. It is possible to pick out some broad patterns in the legal substance of family law cases, and that is all we attempt to do here. It is more difficult to capture the diversity and detail which often give such cases their tortuous, not to say harrowing, character. We should remember, therefore, that the reality is more convoluted than the statistical picture would suggest, even if the statistical picture is useful as a general depiction of key features.

We begin with an account of the opening circumstances of the case — the status of the relationship between the partners when the first approach to the solicitor was made, who took the initiative and whether the partners attended family mediation. We then turn to the substance of the case — the type of legal procedures the parties pursued and the main issues at the centre of those procedures. (The outcome of procedures for those cases in the sample where an outcome had been reached will be dealt with in the next chapter.) The chapter ends with a summary of the main points.

Box 4.1: Marital Separation — A Fictional Sample Case

Spouses: Mary and John, married 16 years, 3 children.
John is a Garda, Mary has a part-time job
as a typist-receptionist in a large garage.

Mary and John have had a long history of conflict over John's heavy drinking and the management of money in the household. As the conflict worsens, Mary eventually decides she wants to separate. When she raises the subject with John, he goes into a rage and tells her not to be talking nonsense. Nevertheless, she sticks with her decision and goes to their family solicitor. She asks him to start proceedings for a judicial separation in the Circuit Court, and to include applications for maintenance and a property order regarding the family home which would favour her and her children. The tensions between Mary and John worsen as the separation case gets underway. Six weeks after John receives the first communication from her solicitor, following some intense bouts of quarrelling, John moves out. He goes to live with his widowed mother, who is living on her own not far away.

The separation case makes slow progress for the first two months. John at first refuses to contact a solicitor, though eventually, when Mary's solicitor writes to him directly, he does so. Even so, it will take at least a further six months before the case gets into the Circuit Court, and then may face lengthy adjournments and delays before it is finalised. Mary therefore applies to the District Court for a maintenance order, since John is making almost no contribution to the children's expenses even though he has a reasonable salary and is getting more-or-less free accommodation from his mother. Mary's maintenance application is heard in the District Court four weeks later and she gets a maintenance order for £70 per week. John is further embittered by what he sees as her heavy handed approach but he pays regularly for the first few weeks. Thereafter the payments are often late and soon become sporadic. Mary begins to threaten that she will go back to the District Court to seek an attachment of earnings order (that is, an order to have the £70 per week deducted at source from John's pay).

Box 4.1 (continued)

After he moves out to his mother's house, John gradually becomes reconciled to the idea of separation but he rejects many of the terms of settlement his wife is asking for. He keeps up a good deal of contact with the children, especially with their oldest boy, Tim, who is 14. He begins to indicate that he wants custody of Tim, arguing that Tim gets on better with him than with his mother, that he and the grandmother could provide Tim with a good home, and that he has brought his drinking under control. Mary is horrified and alarmed at this prospect — she does not want to lose Tim, she thinks Tim's leaning towards his father is simply rebelliousness against her which will soon evaporate, she feels John is hopeless at looking after children, and, in any event, while John insists his desire for custody is genuine, she is convinced he is really doing it out of a desire to hurt her. John, however, insists that his desire for custody is sincere and is in the best interests of the boy. In addition, he finds out that Mary has started to suffer from depression and has begun to take medication. He threatens to use that as evidence of her inability to handle all three children on her own.

It is now seven moths since Mary first went to her solicitor. The case has become highly embittered and stressful for everyone. Mary especially is beginning to crack under the pressure of minding the children and running the house on her own, along with the stress and worry of the separation case. She finally decides to offer a compromise to John: she will drop the maintenance claim if he agrees not to go ahead with the custody application for Tim, to transfer the house into her sole name and to make the remaining mortgage payments on the house (the mortgage has four years to run). Eventually, after much negotiating between their solicitors, John agrees to the deal except that, as far as the family home is concerned, he is willing to concede only that she would have right of residence until their youngest child is 18, at which point the house should be sold and the proceeds divided between them. Mary digs in on this point and the ensuing arguments drag on for another two months — though, to Mary's relief, the custody issue appears to have gone off John's agenda. In the meantime, John's mother is becoming more and more sympathetic to Mary's case, and under pressure from her, John agrees to Mary's demands on the house. The agreement is finalised a week before their case is due to be heard in the Circuit Court. Their solicitors take it to court and have the terms of the agreement read out as an order of the court.

Box 4.1 (continued)

The case has taken 12 months, has left Mary in a state of exhaustion, and has thrown the children's lives into turmoil. Mary and John now face bills for legal costs of over £2,000 each, though it will be long before these are paid. However, the case is now concluded, an air of normality resumes and the family sets about coping with their new circumstances as best they can.

Opening Circumstances of Cases

Status of Relationship

As we saw in the previous chapter, the vast majority of the solicitors' clients in our sample were married to their partners, while a minority were in various forms of cohabitation or non-cohabiting relationships. Table 4.1 shows what the status of these partnerships was when clients first approached the solicitor about their case. The table distinguishes between married and non-married clients though the number of non-married clients is too small to serve as anything more than an indicative sample. In general, clients were most likely either to be still living with each other (43 per cent) or informally separated (37 per cent), while a small proportion (3 per cent) were living together but with a protection order in place.

Certain differences emerge between private and legal aid clients on these issues. Over half of the private clients who were in a marital relationship were still living with their spouses while this was true of only one-third of legal aid clients. This difference may reflect delays in getting free legal aid: where private clients can engage a solicitor's services almost as soon as the decide to take action, legal aid clients may have to wait weeks or even months, within which period an informal separation has more time to take place.

Legal aid clients, on the other hand, were more likely already to have had their spouses excluded by a barring order (13 per cent). This was true of only 2 per cent of private clients. Taking barring orders and protection orders together, it appears that about one in seven of legal aid clients had already either initiated or completed barring procedures before approaching the solicitor while this was true of only one in twenty of private clients.

Table 4.1: Status of Client's Relationship with Partner at First Consultation with Solicitor (in %)

Status of Relationship	Married Clients		Non-married Clients	All Clients
	Private	Legal Aid		
Living together (no orders)	52	32	18	43
Living together (protection order in place)	3	3	—	3
Informally separated	35	38	50	37
Barring order in place	2	13	—	5
Desertion	4	4	—	3
Legally separated	2	4	—	3
Divorced in another country	1	2	2	1
Other	1	5	30*	5
Total	100	100	100	100
(N)	(333)	(129)	(40)	(506)

The incidence of protection and barring orders among clients suggests two things. The first arises from the relatively small proportion of clients in the sample who already have a barring order or protection order in place when they first approach the solicitor. We saw in Chapter Two that barring applications have long been the single most common form of legal proceeding taken by applicants in the Irish family law system. We would therefore expect barring procedures to loom large in solicitors' family law case-files, either because clients already had obtained a protection or barring order before approaching the solicitor or had come to the solicitor in order to obtain one. We now see that relatively few clients have a protection or barring order when they first come to the solicitor. We will examine further below to what extent clients request their solicitor to initiate barring procedures after they make contact. However, we have here a first indication that barring procedures do not loom as large in solicitors' case-files as they do in court applications, thus reinforcing the view that many barring proceedings take place without the benefit of legal representation.

The second, and associated, implication is that recourse to barring orders has an association with social disadvantage: while applications for barring orders may arise at all social levels, they are more likely to occur among the less well-off, that is, in the present instance, among those who cannot afford private solicitors.

Initiative and Response

The question of who initiates the recourse to law — that is, which partner takes the initiative in approaching a solicitor and getting legal action under way — is a further revealing aspect of the opening circumstance of family law cases. We get a first indication on this issue by looking at the gender balance in our sample of solicitors' clients: 61 per cent of the sample are women compared to 39 per cent men (Table 4.2). To examine the nature of this gender imbalance further, we asked solicitors whether they considered that their clients were taking the initiative (initiators) or were responding to an initiative taken by the other party (respondents). The results suggested not only that women were more likely to contact the solicitor than men, but that they were also more likely to do so as initiators rather than in response to an initiative taken by their partners. Eighty-three per cent of female clients in the sample were initiators and a further 4 per cent were joint initiators, while only 37 per cent of male clients were initiators and 8 per cent were joint initiators. Conversely, 55 per cent of male clients were respondents compared to only 13 per cent of female clients.

Female-initiated cases are represented not only by female initiators but also by male respondents — the latter equally imply cases where the woman has taken the initiative. We need to take this into account in estimating the proportion of cases initiated by women. There are 257 female initiators in the sample plus 109 male respondents, making a total of 366 female-initiated cases. This represents 72 per cent of cases in the sample (Figure 4.1). By a similar addition procedure, we get 112 male-initiated cases (73 male initiators plus 39 female respondents), which represents only 22 per cent of cases. Twenty-five cases in the sample (5 per cent of the total) are jointly initiated, while a further four cases (less than one per cent) are initiated under pressure from a third party (such as a building society). In other words, women are more than three times more likely to take the initiative in bringing family conflicts to law than are men, and only in a small proportion of cases do the partners take the initiative together.

Table 4.2: Sex of Clients by Role of Client as Initiator or Respondent

Sex of Client	Role of Client			Total	%
	Initiator	Respondent	Joint Initiator / Other		
Female %	83	13	4	100	61
(N)	(257)	(39)	(12)	(308)	(308)
Male %	37	55	8	100	39
(N)	(73)	(109)	(17)	(199)	(199)
All %	65	29	6	100	100
(N)	(330)	(148)	(29)	(507)	(507)

Figure 4.1: Which Partner Takes the Initiative in Bringing the Case to Solicitor

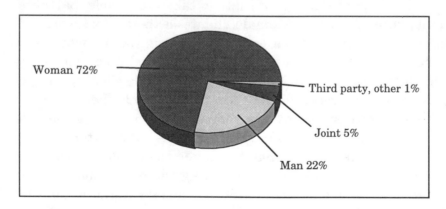

Woman 72%

Third party, other 1%

Joint 5%

Man 22%

A further implication can be drawn from these patterns of initiative and response. This concerns the degree to which a woman or man who takes the initiative in contacting a solicitor is likely to have his or her partner respond by doing likewise. If one partner's initiative in contacting a solicitor were always matched by a response in kind from the other partner, we would expect to have a half-in-half divide between initiators and respondents in our sample. In fact, initiators outnumber respondents in the sample by over two to one (65 per cent to 29 per cent — Table 4.2). Although women dominate among the initiators, the imbalance between initiators and respondents occurs also in that minority of cases where men take the initiative. There are 73 male initiators in the sample but only 39 female respondents. Allowing for the effects of sampling error, the imbalance between initiators and respondents is therefore roughly of the same order for both male and female initiators. While women are more likely to take the initiative in family law cases, and so are more likely to have partners who do not respond in like manner, in the minority of cases where men take the initiative, it is almost as likely that their partners will not contact a solicitor.

The significance of this pattern is not at all clear. In adversarial family law proceedings, non-co-operation by the responding partner in the form of refusal to engage a solicitor's services is one possible means of resistance. On the other hand, it may sometimes indicate complete absence of resistance: the responding partner may not wish to contest an application and may leave the field open to his or her partner by not seeking legal representation to advance his or her case. The high levels of non-contacting of solicitors probably reflects a mix of these quite different circumstances.

It is also possible that some of the imbalance we have noted is an artefact of the data, in that either clients mislead solicitors or solicitors mislead themselves in regard to who is taking the initiative. However, the question of who is taking the initiative is not entirely a matter of subjective perception since initiative is usually indicated in behavioural terms by which side is first to issue correspondence or other documents, something which solicitors would likely be quite well aware of. Furthermore, the sex distribution in the sample is not subject to mis-reporting error but suggests a real imbalance in the extent to which women rather than men are likely to approach a solicitor. Non-response by the partners of those who initiate family law proceedings therefore needs to be investigated further in order to establish how widely it occurs, why it occurs and what implications it has for the conduct of family law cases.

Role of Mediation

As mentioned in Chapter Two above, attendance at family mediation is increasingly regarded as a useful prelude or adjunct either to adversarial court proceedings in family law cases or to negotiation of settlements through lawyers. The Judicial Separation and Family Law Reform Act, 1989 obliges solicitors to suggest mediation to clients seeking judicial separation and allows courts to adjourn hearings to facilitate mediation. To what extent do solicitors' clients in family law cases attend mediation?

In the present sample, as Figure 4.2 shows, one-third of private solicitors' clients attended family mediation while only one in eight of legal aid clients did so. Attendance at mediation, therefore, is still a minority experience, but in so far as it occurs it is concentrated among those able to afford private legal services. A state-funded family mediation service is so far available only in Dublin, where it was instituted on a pilot basis in 1986. Private mediation is more widely available throughout the country. We could find no evidence in the sample of regional patterns in attendance at mediation, though the number of those in the sample who had attended mediation was too small to allow for conclusive analyses along these lines.

Figure 4.2: Percentage of Solicitors' Clients Who Attended Mediation

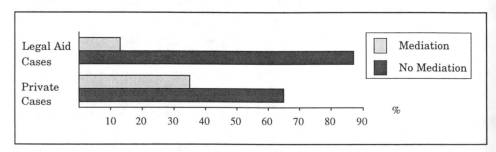

Legal Issues

We now turn to the issues that are at the centre of family law cases in the sample and the legal procedures which the litigants invoke.

Court Level

As we saw in Chapter Two, one basic way of indicating the legal substance of family law cases is to determine which court level they are oriented to. The two main possibilities are the District Court and Circuit Court. These two possibilities are not completely distinct, since many cases might appear at both those court levels, either because of appeals from the District Court to the Circuit Court or because more immediate remedies are sought in the District Court before the case is taken to the slower-moving mechanisms of the Circuit Court. In addition, a certain proportion of cases might be expected to be oriented to the High Court, either by way of an appeal from the Circuit Court or in order to obtain remedies which are not available in the lower courts (such as civil annulment of marriage). A certain number of cases are not oriented to any court level, in that they are aimed to achieve an out-of-court separation agreement. One of our concerns is to establish what proportion of cases fall into that latter category, since no national data are available on the incidence of separation cases which are settled in this way.

Table 4.3 sets out the distribution of the solicitors' case-file sample by court level, based on actual outcomes among concluded cases and on solicitors' best judgement about the most likely outcome in non-concluded cases. The most common orientation of cases is towards the Circuit Court alone (40 per cent), while a further 13 per cent are or were oriented both to the District Court and Circuit Court. Putting these two categories together, over half the cases were either exclusively or partly oriented to the Circuit Court. Only 20 per cent of cases were oriented to the District Court alone. This degree of concentration on the Circuit Court in the sample is high, given what we saw from national statistics in Chapter Two about the dominance of the District Court in family law business. The explanation largely lies in the nature of the sample: as mentioned already, it consists of legally represented cases only and so does not cover the large proportion of District Court cases which have no legal representation.

Table 4.3: Court Level of Cases by Type of Legal Representation (in %)

	Private	*Legal Aid*	*All Cases*
District Court only	16	29	20
District and Circuit Courts	14	12	13
Circuit Court only	40	40	40
High Court	5	5	5
No court	20	9	17
Other combination	5	5	5
Total	100	100	100
(N)	(355)	(151)	(506)

We should also note from Table 4.3 that 20 per cent of private cases and 9 per cent of legal aid cases were not oriented to any court. They were aimed rather at an out-of-court settlement. The lower incidence of out-of-court settlements among legal aid cases is in keeping with their lower rate of attendance at mediation which we noted earlier. It may also in part reflect a selection mechanism in the demand for legal aid. Court-oriented cases are more likely to apply for legal aid since they are more likely to face expensive court procedures. Having obtained legal aid, clients may also be more willing to go to court, since the legal costs of doing so will not fall on them. Out-of-court cases, on the other hand, may only require a solicitor's services to convert the terms of separation agreed by the couple into legal form — something which might be relatively inexpensive and therefore affordable even by less well-off couples. The delay and difficulty in getting legal aid may provide an additional incentive to those who are on the margins of agreement to keep to the consensual path as much as possible rather than to turn to the courts. Many of those who do not qualify for legal aid may be unable to afford the legal costs of a full hearing, thus increasing the likelihood that they will settle by agreement.

The statistics on court proceedings which we reviewed in Chapter Two above do not provide coverage of out-of-court cases, so we should regard this category of solicitors' family law business as an addition to the counts of family law cases which we estimated in Chapter Two. We will take this category into account when we attempt to estimate the overall incidence of marital breakdown in Ireland in Chapter Five below.

For those cases which do go to court, private cases are less likely to be oriented to the District Court than are legal aid cases. This is in keeping with our earlier suggestion that barring and associated procedures, and thus an orientation to the District Court, is associated with social disadvantage. Agreed settlement of cases, perhaps with the aid of mediation, is more likely to be routed through private solicitors, partly because of the selection mechanisms we have just mentioned but also perhaps because better-off couples are more likely to have the resources which facilitate agreement (such as the ability to afford private mediation).

Relationship to Legal Separation

We can next provide a broad categorisation of cases by determining whether they were oriented towards legal separation or not. The possibilities here are, first, that the client is not married to the other party, so that the question of legal separation does not arise; second, that the parties are married but they are seeking some remedy other than legal separation, and finally that they are married and are seeking a legal separation. Again, we should recall the simplifications on these questions which our data may entail: it is not always clear what the real demands or expectations of the partners might be, so that the distinction between, say, separation and non-separation cases is not always as clear-cut as it might appear. Our data on this issue represent the best judgement of solicitors on the basic nature of cases rather than a clearly evident set of distinctions.

Table 4.4 shows that, while the great majority of cases are pursuing legal separation, a significant minority have different concerns. Over 80 per cent of private cases are geared towards legal separation, 12 per cent involve married couples who are seeking something other than legal separation and six per cent involve non-married partners. Legal aid cases have a higher representation of non-marital partnerships (15 per cent) and of non-separation cases among married partners (24 per cent).

We can understand the orientation of cases to legal separation somewhat better by considering whether the initiator of the case in each category was male or female (see Table 4.5; the number of cases in the non-marital and marital non-separation categories in this table are small, so that the breakdowns within them are subject to wide sampling errors). In keeping with what we suggested about patterns of family law in the District Court in Chapter Two above, non-marital cases in the solicitor's case file sample have a high incidence of male initiators — almost a half in the present instance. This reflects the prominence of guardianship procedures taken by unmarried fathers in these kinds of cases. Non-separation cases involving married couples also have a marginally higher than usual incidence of male initiators (24 per cent).

Table 4.4: Relationship to Separation by Type of Legal Representation (in %)

Relationship to Separation	Private	Legal Aid	All Cases
Non-marital (non-separation)	6	15	8
Marital — non-separation	12	24	16
Marital — separation	82	62	76
Total	100	100	100
(N)	(353)	(151)	(504)

Table 4.5: Relationship of Case to Legal Separation by Gender of Initiator (in %)

Gender of Initiator	Relationship to Separation		
	Non-marital	Marital Non-separation	Marital Separation
Female	47	70	75
Male	49	25	18
Joint/Third Party	4	5	7
Total	100	100	100
(N)	(45)	(79)	(386)

Table 4.6 picks out those cases which are oriented towards legal separation and examines the issues which solicitors reported as substantial concerns in the proceedings. The first item to consider is the form of separation which, in the solicitor's view, the parties were most likely to achieve. The possibilities are, first, a separation agreement (that is, an agreement formalised by means of a deed of separation drawn up by the solicitors for the two sides without going to court); secondly, a judicial separation order (that is, where the question of separation and issues associated with it — maintenance, access, custody, etc. — is decided by the court); and thirdly, a judicial separation order by consent (that is, a judicial separation which has been agreed in advance by the parties and which the judge simply reads into the record of the court). The percentage distribution across these categories adds up to slightly over 100 per cent because in a small number of cases, solicitors were unsure which outcome was most likely and so mentioned more than one.

Table 4.6: Issues in Cases Seeking Legal Representation (Married Clients Only) (% mentioning each item)*

Issues	*Private*	*Legal Aid*	*All Cases*
Separation:	100	100	100
Separation agreement	(50)	(36)	(46)
Judicial separation order	(32)	(53)	(37)
Separation order by consent	(20)	(18)	(19)
Ancillary issues:			
Property issues	83	67	79
Maintenance — spouse	66	48	62
Maintenance — children	67	47	63
Access to children	54	56	58
Custody of children	53	67	54
Barring orders	28	48	33
Foreign divorce	2	2	2
Civil nullity	1	1	1
Other	2	8	3
(N)	(290)	(93)	(383)

* Percentages do not always add to 100 because of multiple mentions of items.

From Table 4.6 it is clear that, in the sample as a whole, separation agreements are the most common of the three possibilities: 46 per cent of all cases have achieved or, in the solicitor's view, are likely to achieve this outcome, compared to 37 per cent for judicial separation orders and 19 per cent for separation orders by consent. However, there is a substantial difference between private and legal aid cases on this question: over half of private cases are aimed towards this form of settlement, compared to less than one-third of legal aid cases. Legal aid cases are much more likely to require a judicial separation. Indeed, in private cases, it is striking to note that, if we add together those oriented towards separation agreements and those oriented towards judicial separations by consent, then we have a total of about 7 out of every ten cases which are settled by consensual agreements. Less than one-third require judicial decision. Among legal aid cases, the ratio between consensual separations and those requiring judicial decision is closer to half-and-half.

Overall, therefore, the incidence of consensual separation is quite high. In fact, it is a good deal higher than the incidence of non-court oriented cases which was reported above in Table 4.3 (which was only 20 per cent for private cases and 9 per cent for legal aid cases). This suggests that many consensual separations are consensual only at the end: they may have gone through court proceedings (for example barring or maintenance proceedings in the District Court) at earlier stages in the case and arrived at agreement on overall terms of separation only after a long struggle. It reminds us not to assume that consensus in this context equates with civility and reasonableness between the partners. Rather, it may emerge in the manner of a peace treaty at the end of a long and bitter war — either because one side admits defeat or because both sides are so exhausted that they cannot continue the fight (see the sample case outlined in Box 4.1 above).

Ancillary Issues

When we look at the ancillary questions which are dealt with in legal separation cases, property issues are the most prominent: 83 per cent of private cases and 67 per cent of legal aid cases have these as a substantial concern. The family home is usually the central concern in negotiations over property and because of its centrality in family law cases, we will deal with it in more detail in the next chapter when we look at the outcome of cases.

Maintenance for spouses and children is the next most common issue, though less so for legal aid cases than for private cases. We will deal with this question further below in the chapter on outcomes. Questions of custody and access in relation to children come next in frequency. We will outline in the next chapter which parent children end up living with after cases are concluded, but we have not attempted to trace the complex conflicts, negotiations and settlements that often accompany the custody and access aspects of family law cases.

Overlap between Barring and Separation Cases

Barring orders also arise in a substantial proportion of marital separation cases, though much more so in legal aid cases than in private cases. Barring orders were an issue in almost half of the legal aid cases in Table 4.6 compared to just over a quarter of private cases. In some of these cases, the barring order was already in place when the client came to the solicitor, but in the majority it was dealt with after consulting with the solicitor. It appears also that in something less than half of these cases, the question of barring arose by way of a barring application to the District Court but in slightly more than half it was included as part of separation proceedings in the Circuit Court.

This suggests two important implications as far as our characterisation of the overall structure of the family law system is concerned. First, it indicates that the barring/protection function of the system described earlier is expressed not only through barring/protection applications in the District Court but also, on a much smaller scale, as part of composite separation applications in the Circuit Court. Thus, in attempting to estimate the incidence of family law cases where violence and abuse on the part of one of the spouses is an issue in the legal proceedings, we should add a small proportion of separation cases in the Circuit Court to the count of barring cases in the District Court. This has the effect of increasing even further what we earlier characterised as the large proportion of family law cases in the system where violence and abuse play a central role.

The second implication we should draw relates to the size of the overlap between separation cases and barring/protection cases. In Chapter Two, we noted from national family law statistics that the volume of barring applications in the District Court exceeded the volume of separation applications in the Circuit Court by a wide margin. This imbalance between the two segments of the system means that if applicants for barring orders normally followed through by seeking a fully fledged legal separation, legal separation cases in the Circuit Court would be dominated by those who already had a barring order from the District Court or who sought one in the early stages of the separation case. In fact, we see now that, while there is some overlap of this kind, it is quite small. This is so particularly when we recall that in more than half the cases where barring is an issue in separation cases, it arises as a new issue in the Circuit Court rather than as a carry-over from the District Court. Thus we have evidence here that, apart from this small element of overlap, the barring and separation segments of the family law system apply to largely different clienteles and thus differ not only in function but also in the people they deal with.

Issues in Non-separation Cases

In Table 4.7 we turn to those cases which were not substantially geared to legal separation. As we saw from Table 4.4 above, one-third of these cases involved unmarried persons for whom the question of legal separation could not arise, while the remainder involved married persons. Among the married clients, many cases involved existing separations where the client was seeking alterations to aspects of existing arrangements which he or she found unsatisfactory. Others involved new cases where the client was seeking one or more District Court remedies. The number of cases in these categories is too small to allow for detailed analysis but for indicative purposes the table sets out the issues which comprised them, distinguishing between married and non-married clients (see also Table 4.10

at the end of the chapter which classifies the issues in non-separation cases by private and legal aid clients).

Table 4.7: Issues in Non-Separation Cases by Marital Status of Clients (% mentioning each item)*

Issues	Married Clients	Unmarried Clients	All Clients
Property issues	30	9	22
Maintenance — spouse	29	n/a	19
Maintenance — children	34	38	35
Access to children	40	58	46
Custody of children	34	22	30
Appointment of guardian	n/a	42	16
Barring orders	30	n/a	21
Foreign divorce	9	n/a	6
Paternity test	n/a	16	6
Civil nullity	17	9	14
Other	3	13	7
(N)	(76)	(45)	(121)

*Percentages do not add to 100 because of multiple mentions of items.

For married clients, all of the major issues occur with similar frequency, though at a lower level than in the case of separation cases. Access to children is the more common by a small margin, but property, maintenance, custody and barring orders also feature. Civil nullity proceedings in the High Court arise in 17 per cent of the cases. For unmarried clients, access to children is the most common proceeding, followed by applications for appointment as guardian. The applicants in these cases quite often are unmarried fathers. Maintenance for children is also common, but maintenance for spouses, like barring applications, does not figure at all in non-marital cases since the law at present does not allow for an unmarried mother to seek a maintenance for herself (as opposed to her children) from her partner.

Role of Children

As we saw in the previous chapter, 79 per cent of clients in the sample had dependent children. We have also seen at various points that issues connected with children — custody, access, appointment of guardian (in the case of unmarried fathers) and maintenance for children — are among the most common issues to arise in family law cases. However, this of itself does not tell us to what extent children are a focus of conflict in family law cases. In some instances, this issue is quite clear-cut. Children may be either at the centre of conflict (in cases, for example, where conflict about custody or the forms or degree of access the non-custodial parent should have is the key issue in dispute) or they may not be a matter of dispute at all (for example, in cases where the departing husband has no interest in the children and the entire conflict is about division of property, or where the children may be grown up and living their own lives independently).

More usually, however, where there are dependent children they can be a focus of conflict to varying degrees and in a wide variety of ways. For example, one partner may resist the other partner's request for separation for the sake of the children, a conflict over which partner should have the family home may be tied in with a conflict over custody, the children might take sides between their parents in aspects of the conflict which are not focused directly on them, and so on. The range of possible variations and the difficulty in categorising them were so great that we did not attempt to explore the issue in any detail. Rather, we settled for an overall general assessment of the extent to which, in the view of the solicitor supplying the information, the children were a focus of dispute in the case.

We first consider this issue with reference to the marital status of the client (Table 4.8). Although the number of unmarried clients in the sample is too small to allow for detailed breakdowns, it is clear from the data that the incidence of conflict over children among those clients is very high, arising in either a major or secondary way among 36 out of the 42 cases. This in part reflects the selective nature of the family law system: proceedings involving unmarried persons arise almost solely with reference to their children, since legal provisions dealing with the partners themselves (such as separation, division of property, maintenance of spouses, barring procedures) do not apply to unmarried persons. In addition, it is notable that the type of focus on children which arises in cases involving unmarried partners is almost entirely conflictual. In looking at national statistics on family law proceedings between unmarried partners in Chapter Two, we raised the possibility that some of those proceedings might have a family building character: unmarried couples in stable unions might use guardianship procedures to strengthen the man's legal relationship with their children. Here, however, it appears that such a situation occurs at most only rarely.

Table 4.8: Extent of Dispute about Children by Marital Status of Clients (in %)

Extent of Dispute	Clients with Dependent Children		All Clients
	Unmarried	Married	
Major focus of dispute	74	36	31
Secondary but significant focus of dispute	12	23	17
Minor focus of dispute	5	18	13
Not in dispute at all	10	24	18
No dependent children	—	—	21
Total	100	100	100
(N)	(42)	(354)	(510)

Among married clients with dependent children, the children were a major or secondary focus of dispute in almost 60 per cent of cases, while they were not in dispute at all in almost one in four of cases. In the sample as a whole, when we include clients with no dependent children, the proportion where children are a major or secondary focus of dispute drops to just under a half.

It is also of interest to consider the degree of dispute about children according to the type of separation which couples are pursuing. Table 4.9, which picks out separation cases where the couples have dependent children, shows that there is some tendency for the level of dispute about children to be lower among those with agreed separations compared to those requiring court adjudication. However, the differences are not statistically significant, and it is notable that even in the case of separation agreements, children were a major or secondary focus of dispute in half the cases.

Table 4.9: Extent of Dispute about Children by Type of Separation Sought (Couples with Dependent Children Only) (in %)

Extent of Dispute	Separation Agreement	Separation Order by Consent	Separation Order
Major focus of dispute	27	39	38
Secondary but significant focus of dispute	23	19	27
Minor focus of dispute	20	19	19
Not in dispute at all	29	23	17
Total	100	100	100
(N)	(124)	(57)	(117)

This quite high incidence of conflict over children, even among those pursuing separation agreements, reinforces the point made earlier that "agreement" in this context does not necessarily mean absence of conflict, either before or after the agreement is finalised. It often means simply that conflict occurs through mechanisms other than court proceedings, and that it may be resolved through reluctant concessions or a war of attrition rather than through real consensus. "Agreed" separations, therefore, may often be more harmonious and civilised than adjudicated separations but they need not always be so, and it should not be assumed that they will be universally to be more equitable or acceptable to both parties than those imposed by a court.

Conclusion

This chapter has provided an account of certain basic legal features of cases in the solicitors case-file sample. Just over half of the clients in the sample were already living apart when they first approached the solicitor. Only a minority of cases attended family mediation: over a third of private clients did so at some point in the proceedings but this was true of only one in eight of legal aid clients. In the great majority of cases, women took the initiative in bringing the case to a solicitor, though among un-married clients (who formed 9 per cent of the sample), unmarried fathers seeking access to their children were often the initiators. As expected from the nature of the sample, cases were heavily oriented to the Circuit Court. This reinforces the view that family law cases which have legal representation have a different profile than cases as a whole in the family law system, being much less oriented to District Court remedies. A substantial minority of cases (one-fifth of private clients, one-tenth of legal aid clients) had not and did not expect to appear before any court — they were pursuing out-of-court settlements.

The majority of cases in the sample were seeking legal separation (again reflecting the bias towards this part of the family law system among legally represented family law cases). There was a high incidence of agreement-oriented separations, either in the form or separation agreements or separation orders by consent. Seven out of ten separation cases among private solicitors were oriented to such an outcome, compared to half of legal aid cases. It also seems, however, that many agreement-oriented cases did make applications to court in connection with individual issues such as maintenance, access and so on. Of the ancillary issues in legal separation cases, division of property featured most frequently, followed by maintenance — though in legal aid cases, questions of child custody and access arose more frequently than questions of maintenance.

Barring procedures arose in a minority of cases, though not as commonly as one would expect given the large volume of barring applications which is evident from national statistics on family law proceedings. For many of the barring cases in the sample, the question of barring was raised as part of separation proceedings in the Circuit Court rather than as free-standing barring proceedings in the District Court. The data seem to suggest that there is relatively little carry-over between barring cases in the District Court and separation cases — those who apply for barring orders in the District Court generally do *not* go on to seek legal separation, either by agreement or by Circuit Court order.

For the minority of cases in the sample which were not seeking legal separation, about one-third were accounted for by litigation between unmarried partners and two-thirds were accounted for by marital partners seeking remedies on one or two individual issues.

Eight out of ten cases in the sample had dependent children, and for about 60 per cent of these, the children were a substantial focus of dispute. There was no significant difference between private and legal aid cases on this count. Nor was there much difference in the incidence of dispute about children between separation cases oriented to consensual settlement and those oriented to separation by judicial order.

Table 4.10: Issues in Non-Separation Cases (Married and Unmarried Clients) by Private and Legal Aid Cases (by % mentioning each item)

Issues	Private	Legal Aid	All Cases
Property issues	34	9	22
Maintenance — spouse	28	9	19
Maintenance — children	43	27	36
Access to children	43	51	46
Custody of children	31	29	30
Appointment of guardian	12	18	16
Barring orders	20	22	21
Foreign divorce	8	4	2
Paternity test	5	7	6
Civil nullity	8	22	1
Other	2	13	3
(N)	(65)	(55)	(12)

CHAPTER 5

OUTCOMES OF SAMPLE CASES

In this chapter we focus on those cases in the solicitors' case file sample which were concluded or were on the point of being concluded and examine the outcomes of those cases, that is, the settlements which were reached to bring the cases to a conclusion. Solicitors often say that family law cases never conclude — or at least not until one of the partners dies or the children are all grown up. Such is the enduring nature of family conflicts. Nevertheless, solicitors were usually able to speak of a conclusion in cases in the sense that they had come to a major break, with at least a strong possibility that the outcome reached would keep the partners out of litigation for the foreseeable future. It is in this cautious, if rather bleak, sense that we talk of cases being concluded.

Fifty-four per cent of private cases and 47 per cent of legal aid cases in our sample of solicitors' case files were in that category, giving us an effective sample of 262 concluded cases. While this sample is too small to allow for detailed breakdowns, it does enable us to depict some general features of the settlements which were arrived at. We do so in this chapter under four headings — general outcomes, maintenance, disposition of the family home and residence of children. We also present some information towards the end of the chapter on the duration of concluded cases.

General Outcomes

We saw in Chapter Four that not all family law cases handled by solicitors are seeking separation. Many are seeking more limited remedies such as maintenance, custody, access or protection orders. When we look at the general outcomes of cases, this pattern is confirmed — non-separation outcomes account for 17 per cent of concluded private cases and 42 per cent of concluded legal aid cases (Table 5.1). Separation agreements are the most common outcome. When we add separation orders by consent to separation agreements, we see that consensual outcomes account for well over half of private cases and almost one-third of legal aid cases. Adjudicated separations (judicial separation orders) account for only about a quarter of the outcomes.

Table 5.1: General Outcomes of Concluded Cases

Type of Outcome	Private Clients	Legal Aid Clients	All clients
Non-separation outcome	17	42	24
Separation agreement	36	16	31
Separation order by consent	23	16	21
Judicial separation order	24	27	25
Total	100	100	100
(N)	(191)	(71)	(262)

In looking at the distribution of outcomes in Table 5.1 we should note the possibility of sample selection bias. Because of delays and procedural formalities in dealing with adjudicated separation cases in the Circuit Court, non-adjudicated cases are likely to be concluded more quickly and in greater numbers. One consequence is that in a cross-sectional sample of recently concluded cases such as the present one, non-adjudicated cases may tend to be over-represented. If one were to sample instead on a *cohort* basis, that is, to take a random selection of cases which began on a particular week or month and follow them through to conclusion, adjudicated separation might well be more common as an outcome than it is in Table 5.1.

Maintenance

Previous research by Ward (1990) on maintenance arrangements consequent on marriage breakdown in Ireland had suggested two quite strong findings. One was that the amounts of maintenance were very low — 60 per cent were for amounts less than the rate of supplementary welfare allowance, the lowest social welfare payment. The second was that default rates were very high — three-quarters of maintenance orders were in arrears of six months or more and only 13 per cent were up to date.

Though Ward's research was undoubtedly correct in highlighting the inadequacy of maintenance arrangements following marriage breakdown, his findings gave a less than complete view of the patterns involved. The sample of cases he studied was drawn from District Court files and thus did not include maintenance cases in the Circuit Court. Neither did it include maintenance arrangements arrived at by agreement between the partners without going to court. While Circuit Court settlements and out-of-court settlements might have problems of their own, they would be likely to include higher maintenance amounts and might well have lower rates of default (though the latter is by no means self-evident). Ward's data were also limited in that they provided no information on possible compensatory measures which might have substituted for maintenance — for example, the transfer of the family home or other property from one partner to the other. Where a husband leaves the family home and agrees to continue meeting the mortgage payments, that outcome might not be considered as a maintenance arrangement but would have a maintenance effect. We also have to take into account that Ward's research was based on maintenance cases between 1976 and 1986, before the coming into force of the Judicial Separation and Family Law Reform Act, 1989. Various provisions in the 1989 Act (particularly regarding the division of property) strengthen the hand of dependent spouses and so may tend to improve maintenance settlements and their implementation from the dependent spouse's point of view. This is not to say that maintenance is now likely to work effectively but that the pinched and faltering nature of maintenance arrangements may not be as extreme as it was among the cases Ward studied.

We can throw light on at least some of these questions by looking at maintenance arrangements in the solicitors' case

file sample. We can also offer some limited comments on the
extent to which property settlements might have a quasi-
maintenance effect.

The first question to address is whether or not a maintenance arrangement is included as part of the settlement in the
concluded cases in the sample. Among legal aid cases, only 39
per cent had a maintenance arrangement, while among private
cases 65 per cent had a maintenance arrangement (Figure 5.1).
Overall, therefore, there is a substantial minority of 42 per
cent for which no maintenance arrangement is in place. (We
also examined the incidence of maintenance having excluded
those with no dependent children but the patterns were not
significantly different from those just noted.)

**Figure 5.1: Presence of Maintenance Arrangements by Type of
Legal Representation**

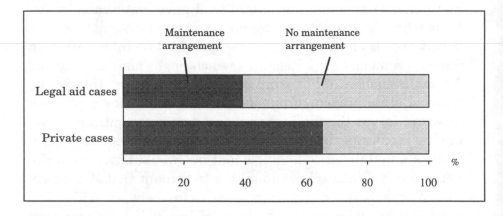

Why might maintenance not be included in settlements? One
possible reason is that the non-custodial parent may have no
job and so may lack the resources necessary to pay maintenance. Alternatively, he may have such a low-paying job that if
he were to pay maintenance his own disposable income would
fall below that which he could obtain on social welfare. In the
latter case, it is unlikely that a maintenance arrangement
would be made since to do so would simply give the man the
incentive to leave his job and go on social welfare. A third possibility is that, rightly or wrongly, neither partner may be

judged to be dependent — they may both have jobs, or a custodial parent (who might normally expect to receive maintenance) may have a job while the non-custodial parent may not.

Our sample of concluded cases was too small to allow for detailed analysis of these possibilities, but we can outline the broad linkages between the employment status of the partners and the presence of maintenance arrangements — see Figure 5.2 (note that the data in this figure relate to number of cases rather than percentages; "work" here means having a full-time paid job; because of the small sample size, data for private and legal aid cases are not shown separately). Maintenance arrangements are most likely to be present when the man has a paid job but the woman does not (the "man works" category in Figure 5.2). They also arise in about two-thirds of the cases where both the man and woman have jobs. Maintenance is most often absent where neither the woman or the man has a job, though there is at least some incidence of non-maintenance across all the categories distinguished in Figure 5.2. Thus it seems that the presence or absence of maintenance arrangements is strongly linked to the employment status of the partners, particularly of the husband, but is not accounted for entirely by this factor.

Figure 5.2: Presence of Maintenance Arrangements by Employment Status of Couple

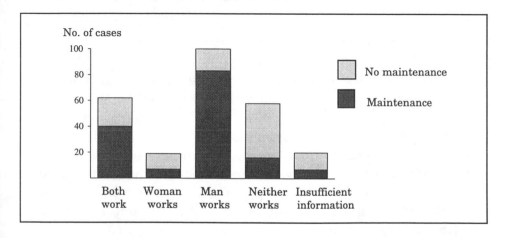

The amount of maintenance payable is shown in Figure 5.3. The two largest payment categories are under £50 per week and £51-100 per week (though in both cases, the boundary sums — £50 and £100 — account for a disproportionate share of those in the category). The median payment per week for private cases is £100 and for legal aid cases it is £60 per week (as there are only 28 cases with maintenance payments in the legal aid sample, the latter figure should be regarded as a very approximate population estimate). Even allowing for inflation since 1986, these sums represent a somewhat higher level of maintenance amounts than was reported by Ward (1990), though they are often still inadequate for the support of a family household.

Figure 5.3: Amounts of Maintenance Payable per Week among Concluded Cases

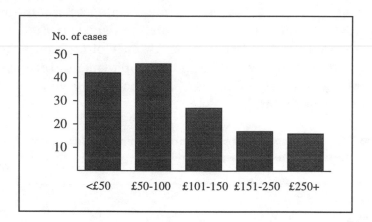

Table 5.2 shows one reason why maintenance amounts in the present sample are higher than those reported by Ward. The median maintenance amounts in Circuit Court cases and "no court" cases (i.e. out-of-court settlements) are more than double those of District Court cases. As already mentioned, the focus of Ward's data on the District Court thus understates the overall level of maintenance payments emerging from settlements. Maintenance amounts were quite strongly correlated with husband's income (correlation coefficient of 0.67).

Table 5.2: Median Amounts of Maintenance Payable per Week among Concluded Cases by Court Level

Court Level	Median Amount (£ per week)	Number of Cases
District Court only	48	26
District Court plus Circuit Court	90	18
Circuit Court only	110	61
High Court	187	7
No court	120	25
All concluded cases	100	148

We can say little about rates of default on maintenance payments from our sample since only recently concluded cases are included. One would expect a low rate of default in the immediate aftermath of the conclusion of the case, since insufficient time would have elapsed for default to emerge. For what it is worth, the vast majority of cases (78 per cent) were reported as up to date with payments, and for many of the remainder the solicitor did not have any information on default one way or the other. However, one would need to track cases in the months and years following their conclusion to assess the real incidence of default. It is also worth noting that, among those cases with a maintenance arrangement in place, an attachment of earnings order had been granted only in a small minority (7 per cent) of cases.

Family Home

As we saw in the previous chapter, the question of the family home was the single most common issue to emerge among separation cases in the sample. Here we can outline how this question was settled among concluded cases. First we can see how many cases included some settlement concerning the family home (Table 5.3). In a substantial minority of cases — half of legal aid cases and 11 per cent of private cases — the family home simply was not an issue. In a further and somewhat smaller minority — 11 per cent of private cases and 16 per cent of legal aid cases — it was an issue but no settlement regarding the family home was included in the outcome. This leaves almost eight out of ten private cases and one-third of legal aid cases where the family home was included in the settlement.

Table 5.3: Family Home in Outcome of Concluded Private and Legal Aid Cases (in %)

	Private	*Legal Aid*	*All Cases*
Family home not an issue	11	49	20
Family home an issue but no settlement reached	11	16	13
Settlement regarding family home included in outcome of case	78	34	67
Total	100	100	100
(N)	(184)	(61)	(245)

The nature of settlements regarding the family home varied a great deal and is difficult to summarise simply. Nevertheless, we can distinguish two aspects of the settlement — residence (who moved out and who stayed on in the family home) and ownership or financial compensation (who benefited and who bore the cost of any financial or ownership implications of the settlement). As far as residence was concerned (Figure 5.4), by far the most common arrangement was that the husband moved out (61 per cent of cases). The wife moved out in 18 per cent of cases, while in a further 16 per cent both moved out and the home was disposed of. These outcomes sometimes overlapped — for example, the husband might move out, leaving the family home to his wife and children, and some time later, she might sell the home in order to get a smaller place or move closer to her own family.

Figure 5.4: Residence Arrangements in Settlements Concerning Family Home

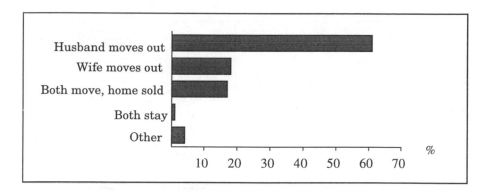

Table 5.4 links the residence outcome with outcomes concerning ownership and financial compensation. Because of the smallness of the number of cases in this table, we reduce the residence outcomes distinguished earlier to two categories — "husband moves out" and "other". The patterns suggest that, whatever the residence outcome, the most likely financial or ownership outcome is that the husband provides some form of compensation to the wife. One common situation is that he moves out and transfers title of the house to her, so that she receives his share of their common equity in the house. Another is that he moves out and continues to pay the mortgage. In a substantial minority of cases, the husband moves out and is compensated by the wife (this occurs in 11 per cent of all cases and 17 per cent of cases where the husband moves out). The most common arrangement here is that she buys out his share of the house. Where the residence outcome is something other than the husband moving out, the most common arrangements are that he stays on and buys out the wife's share or that they sell the house and divide the proceeds. Together, these two options account for nearly nine out of ten cases where the husband does not move out. In a significant minority of cases (12 per cent overall, 19 per cent of cases where the husband moves out), the sale of the house is deferred until some future date (usually when the youngest child is due to come of age), at which point it is sold and the proceeds divided.

Table 5.4: Financial/Ownership Outcome Concerning Family Home by Residence by Residence Outcome among Concluded Cases (in %)

Financial / Ownership Outcome	*Residence Outcome*		
	Husband Moves Out	*Other*	*All*
House sold and proceeds divided	4	44	20
Sale of house deferred	19	2	12
Man compensates woman	47	44	46
Woman compensates man	17	2	11
Other	13	10	12
Total	100	100	100
(N)	(95)	(62)	(157)

It would be of considerable interest to see whether settlements regarding the family home interact with maintenance arrangements — for example, whether calculations of the amount of maintenance payable might take into account arrangements for financial compensation or ownership transfers regarding the family home. There is no doubt that such interactions commonly occur, and may well sometimes be preferred by the dependent spouse to a free-standing maintenance arrangement. On the other hand, under both family law and social welfare law in Ireland, spouses may not contract out of their maintenance obligations. While spouses can, and sometime do, make property settlements in lieu of maintenance, they remain liable to claims for maintenance if the dependent spouse subsequently becomes indigent. In any event, in our sample we could find no clear statistical links between settlements regarding the family home and maintenance arrangements: we did not have sufficient information on the details and value of property settlements to establish if the amount of maintenance was in any way affected by the nature of the property settlement. There was some indication, however, that the two tended to go together: maintenance arrangements were more common where settlements were made regarding the family home.

Residence of Children

The third outcome issue which we can examine concerns residence of dependent children after the break-up of the marriage. We did not gather information on the nature of agreements or court orders concerning such things as formal custody or access arrangements. We concentrated instead on the actual day-to-day outcome as far as living arrangements for the children are concerned. This information provides a good proxy for custody arrangements — the parent whom the children normally live with can be taken as the custodial parent — but it provides no insight on patterns of access by the non-custodial parent.

Table 5.5 presents information on residence arrangements for children in the 218 concluded cases in the sample where the couple had dependent children. This information is classified by whether or not a maintenance arrangement was in place between the partners. By far the most common arrangement is for the children to live with the mother (78 per cent of cases). In an additional small proportion of cases (6 per cent), the parents are still sharing the same house so that the children live with both. Children live with the father in only 5 per cent of cases, and shared arrangements where the children live equally with the father and mother are extremely unusual (2 per cent of cases). It is slightly more common, in fact, to have a split arrangement where some children live mainly with the mother and others live mainly with the father (5 per cent).

The classification by presence of maintenance arrangement shows some link between residence of children and maintenance. The proportion of children living mainly with the mother rises to 87 per cent where there is a maintenance arrangement and it falls to 65 per cent where there is no maintenance. Residence with the father rises to 11 per cent where there is no maintenance.

Table 5.5: Residence Arrangements for Dependent Children among Concluded Cases by Whether Maintenance Arrangements are in Place (in %)

Who Children Live With	Maintenance Arrangement in Place?		All
	Yes	No	
Both parents (still living together)	4	11	6
Mother	87	65	78
Father	2	11	5
Mother and father equally	1	5	2
Neither mother or father	2	5	3
Some with mother, some with father	6	3	5
Total	100	100	100
(N)	(134)	(84)	(218)

Duration of Cases

A common concern about family law cases is that the litigation itself can impose stress on the family over and above the stress of the conflict which give rise to the case in the first instance. One aspect of the stressful nature of such litigation is its tendency to drag on over months. It is difficult to achieve a quick resolution to many such cases, particularly those that involve comprehensive separation proceedings in the Circuit Court rather than one or two individual applications in the District Court.

For present purposes, we define the duration of concluded cases as the interval between the solicitor's first substantial consultation with the client and the most recent such consultation (we exclude incidental contact over things such as payment of fees or routine formalities connected with the finalisation of the case). Table 5.6 confirms that the duration of cases in this sense tends to be long — a median duration of 19 months for private clients and 12 months for legal aid clients. Over a third of private cases went on for two years or more, while a quarter lasted more than 3 years. Legal aid cases tended to be shorter in general — almost 30 per cent lasted for less than six months — but a substantial minority were quite long.

Table 5.6: Duration of Concluded Cases by Type of Legal Representation (in %)

Duration	Private	Legal Aid	All
3 months or less	4	19	8
4-6 months	8	10	8
7-12 months	18	24	20
13-18 months	18	13	17
19-24 months	16	4	12
25-36 months	13	11	13
More than 36 months	24	19	22
Total	100	100	100
(N)	(187)	(70)	(257)
Median duration (months)	19	12	18

The duration of cases is strongly affected by the broad type of legal outcome achieved in the case. As Table 5.7 shows, the median duration of concluded cases increases steadily as we go from non-separation outcomes (12 months), through separation agreements (14 months), separation orders by consent (22 months) and judicial separation orders (30 months).

Table 5.7: Median Duration of Concluded Cases by Type of Outcome

Type of Outcome	Median Duration (months)	Number of Cases
Non-separation outcome	12	62
Separation agreement	14	81
Separation order by consent	22	53
Judicial separation order	30	63
All outcomes	18	259

Conclusion

Legal separation is the most common outcome of family law cases in which solicitors become involved, though a substantial minority have non-separation outcomes. Non-separation outcomes are particularly common among legal aid cases. Among cases with separation outcomes, the three main forms of legal separation — separation agreements, separation orders by consent and judicial separation orders — are more or less evenly represented, though private cases tend to lean more towards separation agreements and legal aid cases more towards judicial separation orders.

About 60 per cent of legal aid cases and one-third of private cases are concluded without a maintenance arrangement. The presence of a maintenance arrangement is strongly influenced by the employment status of the partners — maintenance was most commonly absent where neither partner had a full-time paid job or, to a lesser extent, where both partners had full-time paid jobs. In cases with a maintenance arrangement, the median payment was £100 per week for private cases and £60 per week for legal aid cases. The median payment also varied sharply by the court level at which the case was dealt with, ranging from £48 per week for District Court cases to £110 per week for Circuit Court cases and £120 per week for cases settled out of court.

Settlements regarding the family home were included in almost eight out of ten private cases and one-third of legal aid cases. In these settlements, the most common arrangement was that the husband moved out (over 60 per cent of settlements). Two less common options were that the wife moved out or both moved out and disposed of the family home. Almost half the settlements involved a financial compensation or transfer of some kind from husband to wife — he continued to pay the mortgage while she stayed on in the house or he transferred his ownership interest in the house to her. In a minority of cases, compensation went in the other direction — the wife bought out the husband's share in the home.

Among separated couples with dependent children, the children live with the mother in the great majority of cases (almost eight out of ten). Residence with the father alone is unusual (5 per cent). Shared residence with father and mother equally is quite rare (2 per cent). Split arrangements where some children live with the father and some with the mother are marginally more common (5 per cent).

CHAPTER 6

ESTIMATING THE RATE OF MARRIAGE BREAKDOWN

Public debate about the introduction of divorce in Ireland has often focused on the question of how widespread marriage breakdown is at present. Opponents of divorce say that the incidence of marital breakdown is still low and that therefore the social need for divorce is not pressing enough to warrant lifting the present ban on divorce. Those in favour of legislating for divorce argue that the incidence of marital breakdown is rising rapidly and now affects a sufficiently large minority to justify a fundamental change in the law as far as divorce is concerned.

Some of the conflict on this question reflects ideological differences and a consequent tendentiousness in the way statistical information is interpreted. But it also reflects inadequacies in the underlying statistics — we simply do not have a full and reliable measure of the incidence of marital breakdown. As a result, debate on this question has lacked an adequate informational base. Some information does exist but, as we will see below, it is inadequate as a measure of marital breakdown and is easily open to misinterpretation. The data gathered for this study are insufficient to fill the information gaps which result and do not enable us to provide a definitive estimate of the incidence of marital breakdown. However, they do add to what we know already and they do bring us somewhat closer to a reliable basic picture. The purpose of this chapter is to sketch in that basic picture and thus arrive at a rough estimate of the incidence of marital breakdown, with particular reference to the 1993-94 legal year. It will also make some comparisons with other countries to establish if the rate of marital breakdown in Ireland is high or low by present-day international standards.

Stock and Flow Measures of Marital Breakdown

In order to assess existing statistics on marital breakdown in Ireland, we need to be aware of the distinction between *stock* and *flow* measures. Stock measures count the number of persons (or units of any kind) in a particular category at a particular point in time, flow measures count the number of people who enter a category or make a certain transition over a period of time. The Census of Population is a good example of a stock measure: it counts the number of people in the country on a particular night, and of course also provides counts of the number of people in a wide range of sub-categories (men and women, children and old people, home-owners and renters, urban dwellers and rural dwellers, and so on). The death rate is a typical example of a flow measure: it counts the number of people who make the transition from life to death over a period such as a year. (One way of appreciating the difference between stock and flow measures is to consider that, while flow measures of deaths are commonplace, stock measures of the dead would be difficult to imagine. The latter would entail counting all of those who are presently dead, either by way of a census of the dead or a year-by-year cumulation of the annual totals all those who have died since the beginning of time. Both of these tasks would tax even the most ingenious statistician).

Stocks and flows are related: the number in a particular category at a particular point in time — the stock — is determined by the flows into and out of that category over time. Stocks emerge and grow where the inflow is greater than the outflow, they decline when the reverse happens. Stocks are determined not by the size of inflow but by the difference between inflows and outflows and by the length of time for which that difference has been in place. (Bank accounts provide a familiar example. A small flow of money into one's bank account will eventually amount to a large stock as long as there is little or no outflow. A huge inflow will produce no stock at all if it is counterbalanced by an equally huge outflow — indeed it will become a negative stock if the outflow exceeds the inflow.) We thus have three entities — stock, inflow and outflow — which wholly encompass each other over time. If we know any two of them, we can determine the third (e.g. if we know how much money has gone into our bank account over a given period and how much has gone out over the same period, we can deduce the balance — the stock). However, if we only know one, we cannot deduce the other two. Knowing the stock on its own, for example, will tell us nothing about either inflow or outflow.

These elementary points are worth labouring here since they are often forgotten in talking of the incidence of marital breakdown in Ireland. As we shall see further below, flow statistics on marital breakdown (that is, on the numbers of people making the transition into marital breakdown each year) in Ireland are seriously incomplete, and even at that are not widely available. The result is that much of the debate about the incidence of marital breakdown falls back on stock statistics, particularly those derived from the Census of Population and annual Labour Force Surveys. These statistics can tell us about a number of things, but not about the rate of marital breakdown (i.e. the rate of flow into marital separation). An additional piece of information — statistics on outflow (e.g. through emigration or through formation of second unions) — would be needed to achieve that end on the basis of stock measures. We would also want to take account of time — a large difference between inflow and outflow will produce a substantial stock only if it has been in place for a considerable period of time.

With these caveats in mind, we will first turn to stock measures of those who are separated in Ireland to see what they can tell us about patterns and levels of marital breakdown. We will then turn to flow measures and to what usually is of most concern in debate in this area in Ireland — the rate of marital breakdown.

Numbers of Separated People

The most comprehensive stock measures of marital breakdown in Ireland are those provided by the Censuses of Population in 1986 and 1991. Censuses of Population prior to 1986 used a four-category marital status measure — single, married, widowed and other. The "other" category might have encompassed those who were separated or divorced but in general, because of the limited nature of the measurement categories used, census data prior to 1986 provide little useful information on marital breakdown.

In 1986, and again in 1991, a more elaborate enquiry into marital status was introduced into the Census of Population. All those aged over 15 were first asked to indicate if they were ever married. Those who indicated that they were ever married were then asked to indicate their "present actual marital status, irrespective of the legal status". Nine categories were set out in the Census form to enable people to record their answers, including the five categories for the separated listed in Table 6.1 (the other four categories were married, widowed, remarried following widowhood and remarried following divorce in another country).

Table 6.1: Marital Status of Ever-married Women and Men, 1986 and 1991

Marital Status	Women		Men	
	1986	*1991*	*1986*	*1991*
Married	**653,586**	**667,051**	**650,509**	**662,377**
Separated	**22,607**	**33,793**	**14,638**	**21,350**
Deserted	9,038	16,904	2,584	6,781
Marriage annulled	540	722	443	499
Legally separated	3,888	5,974	3,299	5,178
Other separated	6,792	7,195	6,090	5,787
Divorced in another country	2,169	2,998	2,222	3,105
Total	**676,193**	**700,844**	**665,147**	**683,727**
Separated — increase 1986-91	11,186		6,712	
Annual average increase	2,237		1,342	
Separated as % of total	3.3	4.8	2.2	3.1

Source: Census of Population, Vol. II, 1986, 1991

Two things should be noted about the measure of marital status in the Census of Population. The first is that marital status is self-assessed and self-reported, so that there is considerable scope for people to impose their own definitions on their marital status. The Census form gives no explanation of the meaning of the marital status categories it uses, and this is likely to exacerbate the lack of consistency in how people interpret those categories. In any event, the returns on marital status in both 1986 and 1991 do reveal one notable inconsistency — the number of separated men is a great deal less than the number of separated women. This could reflect the influence of behavioural factors — higher emigration among separated men, or a higher rate of entry into second unions — but it could also reflect a lesser willingness among men to define themselves as separated. In general, the possibility of undercounts of those who are separated in these census measures has to be taken into account. This possibility seems to be considerably greater for men than for women, though it may also be present to some extent for women. We will take the Census data on separated women as a better information source than the corresponding data for men, even though the data on women may fall somewhere short of complete coverage.

The second thing to note about the measure of marital status in recent censuses is the absence of any category for cohabitation without marriage (also often referred to as informal unions, consensual marriages or common-law marriages). This has a bearing on the measure of marital breakdown because it makes it difficult for a man or woman who was previously married but has entered a second informal union to decide how to record himself or herself. Some may count themselves as separated (taking their first marriage as reference point), some may count themselves as married (taking their present relationship as a *de facto* marriage), while others (understandably) may give up on the question and record nothing under this heading. It is not possible to make any useful guess at the effect this feature may have on the resulting data.

The data in Table 6.1 do tell us some interesting things. One concerns the internal composition of the broad category of "separated". In both 1986 and 1991, those who reported themselves as "legally separated" accounted for only a minority of all those who were *de facto* separated (the proportions were about one in five women and one in four men). This may mean that many of those who were *de facto* separated had achieved no legal resolution of their marital status whatever, but it could also mean that many achieved legal resolutions short of legal separation such as barring orders, maintenance orders and so on. In this context, we must again recall that the Census form gave no indication as to how the term "legally separated" should be understood. The low proportion of legally separated among the total separated would support the point made earlier that fully-fledged legal separation is the outcome of only a minority of marriage breakdowns.

Desertion is the largest category of separation for women and is also quite substantial for men. Again, it is not clear how those classifying themselves in this way might have interpreted the term "desertion" so the significance of the numbers involved is not obvious. Most of the overall difference in the numbers of separated men and women arise in this category. In 1991, there were over 10,000 more deserted women than deserted men. The overall difference between the number of separated women and separated men was 12,500 so that the "deserted" category accounted for 80 per cent of the overall difference.

Very few reported themselves as having had their marriages annulled. However, the numbers who were divorced in another country were relatively substantial, amounting to 8.9 per cent all separated women in 1991 and 14.5 per cent of all separated men. This was one category of separation where men outnumbered women.

Changes in Stock Over Time

While stock measures of themselves do not tell us about rates of marital breakdown (for which flow measures are required), changes in the stock over time can provide some useful information on the subject. If we make the assumption that outflow from the separated category is zero over a time period (i.e., that no separated persons emigrated, entered second unions or died over the time period), the increase in the stock indicates how many entered the category over the period. If some people did leave the separated category, the true inflow is correspondingly higher — but never lower — than the net increase in the stock. Changes in the stock can thus give us a lower bound estimate of the numbers of additional separations occurring over the period between the stock measures. Table 6.1 shows that the increase in the stock of separated women between 1986 and 1991 was 11,186, or an annual average of 2,237. This would indicate that the minimum annual average number of marital breakdowns in Ireland over that period was 2,237.

We have no census data for the period since 1991, but the annual Labour Force Surveys provide some indication of trends in the stock of separated persons since then. The Labour Force Surveys are based on a large sample of households rather than on the total population and they do not have the same legal standing as the Census of Population (completing the latter is a legal requirement for every household, whereas participation in the Labour Force Survey is voluntary). The measure of marital status used in the Labour Force Survey is not as detailed as that in the Census of Population, in that it does not distinguish the sub-categories of marital separation in such fine detail. Thus the Labour Force Survey is neither as complete nor as reliable an information source on marital breakdown as the Census of Population. However, it is conducted annually and, at time of writing, data are available up to 1993 so it is worth a brief look.

Table 6.2 shows the numbers of separated men and women estimated by the Labour Force Survey for each year for the period 1986-1993 and also shows the annual increases derived from those numbers. These measures provide a lower count of the separated than do the Census of Population. In 1991, for example, the number of separated women estimated by the Labour Force Survey was 29,600 compared to 33,793 in the Census of Population for the same year. A similar difference arises between LFS and Census of Population measures in 1986. It is not clear why these differences are present — sampling error in the Labour Force Survey may be one reason.

Table 6.2: Estimated Numbers of Separated Women and Men, 1986-93 (in 000s)

Year	Numbers Separated		Change since Previous Year	
	Women	Men	Women	Men
1986	19.3	9.7	n/a	n/a
1987	20.6	11.2	1.3	1.5
1988	24.7	11.9	4.1	0.7
1989	25.0	12.8	0.3	0.9
1990	25.5	14.2	0.5	1.4
1991	29.6	17.1	4.1	2.9
1992	34.2	20.1	4.6	3.0
1993	37.7	20.4	3.5	0.3

Source: Labour Force Surveys, 1986-1993.

Annual increases in the estimated numbers of separated persons in the Labour Force Surveys fluctuate a great deal. In 1988, for example, the estimated increase in the number of separated women since the previous year was 4,100 but it was only 300 the following year. Again, sampling error is likely to account for a large part of these fluctuations. It is unlikely that the actual incidence of marital breakdown would fluctuate from year to year by such a margin. It is somewhat more plausible that net increases in the stock of separated persons (which is what the change data in Table 6.2 show) would fluctuate widely. The net increase is the outcome of two entities — inflows and outflows — which are largely independent of each other and could move in opposite directions from year to year, thus producing large swings in net change.

It does appear from Table 6.2, however, that net increases are consistently higher in 1991 and after than they were in years before then.

Marital Breakdown Rates

To examine the rate of marital breakdown, we turn from stock to flow statistics. The concern is to establish the number of people who enter the state of marital breakdown over a period like a year. In most western countries, statistics are available on the numbers of people making a certain transition (for example, getting a divorce) which can be taken as the key transition in marital breakdown for measurement purposes. In common-sense terms, most people would think that separation of the spouses, that is, when they stop living together, is also a crucial transition in marriage breakdown. However, measures of *de facto* separation of this kind are very rare, since countries generally do not require such transitions to be registered in the way that legal transitions such as a divorce would have to be registered.

In most countries, therefore, flow measures of marital breakdown in effect amount to measures of the divorce rate. In those countries where legal separation is available in addition to divorce, the legal separation rate might be added to the divorce rate to obtain an overall measure of marital breakdown, though simple addition of the two rates might not be appropriate in certain circumstances (if, for example, it entailed a risk of double-counting, where couples might first get a separation and then a divorce). In any event, the most common way of measuring marital breakdown is to focus on those cases that have led to a certain kind of legal resolution — divorce or separation, or some combination of the two.

Here we can define marital breakdown on the same general basis as is usual in statistical measurement in other countries — by including only those cases that have been legally resolved — but this leaves us with the question of which legal resolutions to focus on. We do not have divorce, so reference to that resolution does not arise. We do have judicial separation but, as we have seen, only a portion of marriage breakdowns seek or achieve a full judicial separation. We have separation agreements which do not appear before any court and are not registered in court statistics. In addition, we have the whole range of piecemeal District Court remedies which we have referred to in previous chapters as the largest segment of family law business in the Irish courts. These include not only maintenance, child custody and child access proceedings, but also the numerous category of barring proceedings. Should barring proceedings and other District Court remedies be counted among the legal resolutions to be included in defining what we mean by marital breakdown?

There is no objectively right answer to this question. We will proceed here by taking three different definitions of marital breakdown in order to arrive at estimates of the rate of marital breakdown in Ireland. These are:

1. *Applications* for legal resolution of marital breakdown: these consist of all applications under what has been described earlier as the protection and separation functions of the Irish family law system, including actions for legal separation agreements which do not go to court.

2. *Successful applications*: those applications from 1 which were granted by the courts or, the case of attempts to achieve separation agreements, where an agreement was achieved.

3. *Legal separations*: legal separation agreements and judicial separation orders (i.e. category 2 less cases which achieved a District Court resolution only).

These three definitions exclude what we might call completely informal breakdowns — those cases of marital breakdown which make no application to the family law system whatever — but otherwise range from a broad to a narrow definition of legally resolved marital breakdown.

Drawing on the data examined in Chapter Two, and on the further details of family law cases set out in Chapter Five, we can arrive at a rough estimate of the numbers of new cases of marital breakdown in each of these three senses in the legal year 1993-94. In Chapter Two, we estimated that there were about 5,000 new family law cases in the District Court in that year — 3,000 barring order cases and 2,000 cases seeking other District Court remedies. Of the latter, we estimated that between a quarter and one-fifth involved unmarried couples, so that the number of cases seeking other District Court remedies which need to be considered in connection with marital breakdown has to be reduced accordingly — from 2,000 to about 1,500. There were 2,806 applications for Judicial Separation in the Circuit Court. Of these, about one in eight may also have made applications to the District Court (Chapter Four), so that we will reduce this total by one-eighth (350) to avoid double-counting. This leaves 2,450 applications for judicial separation to be included. In addition, we have to consider separation agreements which are settled out of court. These are difficult to estimate. There appears to about one separation agreement for every separation order (Chapter Five), which would mean that there were about 1,000 separation agreements in 1993-94 (separation orders granted in that year numbered 983). However, a certain proportion of agreed cases seem to make some appearance in court, perhaps to obtain an interim remedy in the District Court which eventually feeds into the overall agreement. To avoid double counting, we will assume that one-fifth of separation agreements are already counted under the District Court statistics, thus reducing the number to be included here to 800.

Table 6.3 brings together the resulting estimates for the three different definitions of marital breakdown. The estimates range from a total of almost 8,000 breakdowns under Definition 1 to less than 1,800 under Definition 3, with Definition 2 in between at 3,335. The corresponding marital breakdown rates per 1,000 population (the "crude breakdown rate") are 2.2 for Definition 1, 0.95 for Definition 2 and 0.51 for Definition 3.

International Comparisons

None of these breakdown rates corresponds exactly to the divorce rate for other countries, since divorce as a marker of breakdown is not available in Ireland. However, the closest approximation is probably the breakdown rate under Definition 2, which is derived from the number of successful applications for legal resolution. While Definition 1 may be better as a proxy for the overall rate of marriage breakdown (including informal as well as legally resolved marriage breakdowns), it is too inclusive to compare with the divorce rate in other countries. Definition 3, on the other hand, is technically closest to a measure of divorce but, as we have seen, under the restrictive conditions of access to separation proceedings in Ireland, it is probably too narrow to serve as a useful international comparison.

Table 6.3: Estimates of Marital Breakdown in Ireland under Three Definitions, Legal Year 1993-94

Type of Case	Definition 1: All Applications	Definition 2: Successful Applications	Definition 3: Legal Separation
District Court barring cases	3,000	1,350	—
Other District Court cases	1,500	1,125	—
Judicial separation* — Circuit Court	2,450	860	983
Separation agreements	800	800	800
Total	7,750	3,335	1,783
Rate per 1,000 population**	2.2	0.95	0.51
Rate per 1,000 married couples**	11.5	4.9	2.64

*Data on judicial separation under Definitions 1 and 2 are adjusted downwards to take account of double-counting with District Court cases, and are re-adjusted upwards under Definition 3 where District Court proceedings are not relevant.
** Base figures from 1991 Census of Population.

Sources: See text.

In order to assess the significance of these breakdown rates, Table 6.4 sets out the crude divorce rates for a selection of high divorce and low divorce countries. Comparing the Irish crude breakdown rate under Definition 2 (0.95 per thousand) to the crude divorce rates for these countries, it would appear that the breakdown rate in Ireland is of a similar order to that of the low-divorce countries of the Mediterranean (these countries have crude divorce rates in the range 0.6 to 1.2 per thousand). In high-divorce countries such as the United States, England and Wales and Sweden, by contrast, the crude divorce rate is a good deal higher, ranging between 2 and 5 per thousand.

Table 6.4: Measures of the Incidence of Marital Breakdown in Selected High-Divorce and Low-Divorce Countries

Country	Year	Crude Divorce Rate (per 1,000 pop)	Divorced / Separated as % of Ever-married (excl. widowed)
High divorce countries:			
United States	1990	4.7	18.1
England and Wales	1989	2.9	10.1
Sweden	1988	2.2	16.6
Low divorce countries:			
Italy	1992	1.2	2.0
Spain	1986	0.6	2.3
Portugal	1989	0.9	1.9*
Greece	1990	0.6	1.6*

* 1981

Sources: Council of Europe Recent Demographic Developments in Europe 1994; United Nations Demographic Yearbook 1987, 1990; Statistical Abstract of the United States 1994; Instituto Nazionale di Statistica, Rome (direct communication).

Table 6.4 also shows the divorced and separated as a percentage of the ever-married population in the selected countries. This indicator is heavily influenced by the rate of re-marriage following divorce and so is not tightly linked to the divorce rate. Sweden, for example, has a lower crude divorce rate than England and Wales but a higher percentage divorced/separated. Nevertheless, the various measures of the incidence of marital breakdown are loosely in line with each other. The percentage divorced/separated ranges from a high of 18 per cent in the United States (the country with the highest divorce rate in the western world) to lows of less than 2.5 per cent in the low-divorce countries of the Mediterranean. The separated in Ireland, according to 1991 Census data, amounted to just under 4 per cent of the ever-married population. This indicator, therefore, places Ireland somewhat above the range of the low divorce countries of the Mediterranean. This probably reflects the absence of the right to re-marry in Ireland, which means that that particular form of exit from the separated category is closed off.

Conclusion

This chapter has looked at various statistical sources in order to examine the sometimes controversial question of the rate of marital breakdown in Ireland. The question is complicated somewhat by the feature of marital breakdown in Ireland noted in earlier chapters and reinforced in this chapter from Census of Population data — the proportion of broken marriages in Ireland which are resolved by means of full legal separation is relatively small. As a result, there are large numbers of separations which are in various degrees of informality or semi-resolution from a legal point of view. Indeed, a substantial proportion of separations are completely informal in that they make no contact with family law at all. This does not make it impossible to estimate the number and rate of marital breakdowns in Ireland but it does make it difficult to compare these estimates with better-defined measures of marital breakdown — such as the divorce rate — in other countries.

Nevertheless, from the rough estimates which are possible, it appears that Ireland has a much lower rate of marital breakdown than the high divorce countries of the western world such as the United States, England and Wales and the Scandinavian countries, but a broadly similar rate to the low-divorce countries of southern Europe — Spain, Portugal, Italy and Greece. Spain was the most recent of these countries to introduce divorce (1981) while the others have had divorce for over two decades (Italy since 1970, Portugal since 1974). The absence of divorce in Ireland, therefore, has not caused Ireland to have a lower marital breakdown rate than is found in southern Europe. It is difficult to say whether the absence of divorce has had some impact in keeping the Irish marital breakdown rate from rising to the levels found in the United States and northern Europe.

CHAPTER 7

CONCLUSION

This study was designed and carried out against a background of widespread lack of knowledge and understanding about the practical operation of the family law system in Ireland, both among policy-makers and the wider public. In seeking to address that lack, the study was constrained by limited research resources and the hitherto unexplored nature of the field. It therefore set itself narrow objectives: it aimed simply to provide a sociological description of certain features of family law in practice in Ireland. The main focus is on the overall structure of the family law system, the types of cases it deals with, the types of clients who take those cases and certain features of the legal outcomes which result. The study points to a number of characteristics of family law practice in Ireland which have attracted little notice before and which need to be investigated thoroughly before we have anything like an adequate informational base for future family law reform. Larger questions about the causes or consequences of marital breakdown, the impact of family law on family life, and the detailed social processes involved in family law cases, were beyond the scope of the study and were not dealt with in any substantial way.

In this chapter, we first summarise the main findings of the analysis and then make some observations on the issues and implications for family law reform which arise from the study.

Main Findings

The analysis has suggested that the overall structure of the family law system in Ireland is characterised by a number of dualisms (see Figure 7.1 for a schematic representation).

Figure 7.1: Schematic Representation of Two-Tier Family Law System

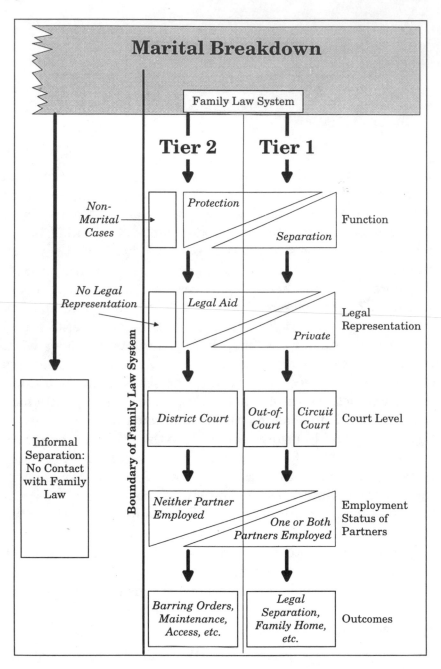

First, family law serves two main functions — protection against spousal violence and marital separation. Secondly, it takes place mainly at two court levels — the District Court and the Circuit Court, with the District Court being the more important of the two as far as numbers of cases dealt with in the courts is concerned. Thirdly, family law cases either have no legal representation at all or are represented by private solicitors, with legal aid solicitors providing a bridging category between these two alternatives. Fourth, the clientele who have recourse to the system tend to cluster around two poles of economic standing — on the one hand, the two-earner couple living in owner-occupied housing, and on the other hand, the social welfare dependent couple with a higher than average likelihood of living in local authority or private rented accommodation or lacking a family home. Finally, the outcomes of cases can be divided between those which achieve comprehensive legal separation and those which achieve a more narrowly-focused resolution dealing with one or two issues which have been of concern to them.

We will now recap the outlines of these dualisms briefly, note the exceptions and transitional cases which blur the boundaries between them and attempt then to assess how far they overlay each other so as to shape the overall nature of the family law system in Ireland.

Dualism of Function

The two major functions of the family law system are *protection* and *marital separation*. The protection function is expressed through barring and protection procedures taken under the Family Law (Protection of Children and Spouses) Act, 1981. Cases which centre on this function are statistically the most common form of proceeding which come before the courts, to the point where one could say that, as far as court-oriented family law cases are concerned, the 1981 Act is the single most important piece of legislation in the Irish family law system. In 1993-94, over 4,500 applications for barring orders were made in the District Court, of which we estimate that about 3,000 were new cases and about 1,500 were repeat cases which had been before the courts before, in connection either with barring procedures or some other type of family law application.

Less than half of barring applications in 1993-94 were granted. It appears that the main reasons for non-granting of applications were either adjournment of the case or non-appearance of the applicant spouse on the day of the hearing (in which case the application is struck out). A third, somewhat less common, reason for non-granting of applications was refusal of the application, usually on the basis of inadequate grounds.

The marital separation function of family law is mainly concerned with the legal regulation of the consequences of non-violent marital breakdown, particularly at the point where one or both of the spouses wants to live apart. It can take any one of three main forms: an out-of-court separation agreement negotiated between the two spouses (in a minority of cases with the aid of family mediation but usually through the solicitors for both sides), separation proceedings in the Circuit Court under the Judicial Separation and Family Law Reform Act, 1989, or piecemeal proceedings in the District Court dealing with discrete aspects of separation — maintenance, child custody and child access especially. Within the court system, taking the District Court and Circuit Court together, the separation function accounts for a somewhat smaller proportion of cases than the protection function. However, when one adds in the separation cases which are resolved without going to court, separation cases outnumber protection cases by a certain margin.

The marital separation function and the protection function overlap in a number of ways. Some of those who seek protection or barring orders in the District Court, for example, go on to seek judicial separation in the Circuit Court; others accompany the barring application in the District Court with other separation-type applications in the District Court, principally for maintenance orders or for orders dealing with the husband's access to children. A certain portion of separation cases in the Circuit Court also include applications for barring orders, so that barring procedures are sometimes incorporated within comprehensive Circuit Court separation proceedings.

However, although overlaps of these kinds exist, they are not particularly common, so that to a great extent, the protection and marital separation functions of the family law system operate as distinct procedures which are applied to different groups of family law cases.

Not all family law cases fit fully under these two main functions. This is true especially of that relatively small but growing category of cases which involve non-married partners. Non-marital litigation is a somewhat marginal part of the system both in a statistical sense, in that the number of family law cases involving non-marital partners is much smaller than those involving spouses, and in a legal sense, in that the range of statutes under which non-marital partners can litigate is much narrower than is the case for spouses. Some non-marital litigation parallels that between spouses, particularly maintenance cases where an unmarried mother may seek financial support for her child or children from the father. Such cases often approximate maintenance proceedings between married persons and could be said to form an extension of the separation function of the family law system. Other types of non-marital cases are more specific to unmarried persons, for example, where an unmarried father seeks to be appointed guardian to his child or children (something which is unnecessary for married fathers since they automatically have rights of guardianship), or where the partners never had a cohabiting relationship. Even these cases, however, often carry echoes of marital separation, especially in that access to children by the father — a common issue in marital separation cases — is often the key issue to be resolved. Cases focused on guardianship and access to children by unmarried fathers have become increasingly important in the family law system since the late 1980s, partly under the influence of the Status of Children Act, 1987. These now form a small but significant minority of all family law cases.

It is worth noting that, at present, the protection function of the family law system is unavailable to non-marital partners. This will change in the future if the recently published Domestic Violence Bill is passed into law. This Bill, among other things, proposes to make barring and protection procedures available to cohabiting couples. The probable consequence will be that procedures of this kind between non-marital partners will become quite numerous and will create a non-marital parallel to the existing protection function of family law for the married population. Given that the system already allows for a non-marital parallel to certain aspects of the marital separation function, this will bring non-marital litigation closer into line with the two-function structure of the family law caseload among the married population.

Dualism of Court Level

Alongside the two-function character of the system, Irish family law is also marked by a two-level court system, arising from the division of jurisdiction for family law cases between the District Court and the Circuit Court (the High Court also enters the picture, but because the number of cases dealt with in the High Court is small, we have not included it within the scope of the present study). In one sense, the Circuit Court is the dominant side in this division, since the extent and flexibility of its powers in dealing with family conflict are greater than those of the District Court. Thus, as far as the protection function is concerned, the Circuit Court can grant long-term barring orders where the District Court can grant such orders only for a maximum term of twelve months. As far as separation is concerned, the Circuit Court can order comprehensive, flexible settlements, embracing not only separation itself but also maintenance orders, child custody and child access orders and property orders (the latter, in particular, are based on quite extensive powers over property relations between separating spouses). The District Court, by contrast, cannot deal with legal separation itself, it cannot adjudicate on the division of property and, on those separation issues it can deal with — maintenance, child custody and child access — it has more limited powers and less scope for flexible, comprehensive settlements than the Circuit Court.

Nevertheless, although the District Court is the lesser of the two jurisdictions from a legal point of view, it is the more important from a practical point of view. This is most clearly so in a statistical sense — the District Court handles about twice as many family law cases per year as the Circuit Court. It also is true in a functional sense: though the District Court's powers in family law are limited, they are used to the full, while many of the Circuit Court's more extensive powers are drawn upon only to a limited extent. In practice, therefore, the District Court has a broader functional role. It is overwhelmingly responsible for the exercise of the protection function of the family law system (the Circuit Court's role in this area is statistically quite minor). The District Court is also extensively involved in the marital separation function, despite the limited nature of its powers in this area — extensive use is made of its powers to deal with maintenance, custody and access issues. Furthermore, the District Court is almost exclusively responsible for dealing with non-marital litigation. The Circuit Court, by contrast, is largely concentrated on one function, marital separation. Although its jurisdiction in this area is legally comprehensive and powerful, the number of cases it actually processes is relatively small. As already mentioned, it plays only a minor role in the protection function, despite the strength of its powers in this area. It plays almost no role in litigation between unmarried partners.

The key feature of the District Court which accounts for its importance in the system is its accessibility. District Court procedures are relatively simple — in many cases there is no need to involve solicitors, costs are comparatively low (in fact, in many cases, there are no financial costs at all) and proceedings can often be completed in weeks rather than in months. In the Circuit Court, by contrast, procedures are more formal and elaborate, representation by solicitors (and usually barristers) is essential, costs are therefore likely to be substantial (and for many, this means that legal aid must be obtained), and in many circuits extensive backlogs in the lists of family cases add months of delay to the processing of cases. In legal terms, the Circuit Court may be the more adequate forum for the handling of family law cases, since it has the legal powers and procedures needed to perform that task thoroughly. In practice, it is ponderous and slow, it cannot really be accessed without professional legal assistance and it lacks the judges, courtrooms, backup staff and other facilities necessary to handle the volume of business it is confronted with.

Taking the statistical and functional patterns of District Court and Circuit Court jurisdictions together, we could speak of a tiered structure in the court system as far as family law is concerned. The District Court provides the broad functional and statistical base of the system, the Circuit Court provides the narrower, more concentrated upper level (for completeness, one could refer to the High Court as the peak of the system). There is a certain region of interpenetration between the two tiers, mainly represented by cases which begin with individual applications in the District Court before eventually going on to seek a more comprehensive separation settlement in the Circuit Court. However, apart from limited overlap of this kind, it is the separateness of the two levels which is more striking than any interconnections between them.

Dualism of Legal Representation

A further dualism one can identify in the family law system is that between cases in which solicitors (and possibly barristers) become involved and those in which they do not — that is, between legally represented and legally unrepresented cases. The latter arise almost exclusively in the District Court and are initiated on the clients' behalf by District Court clerks. We estimate that about half of family law cases in the District Court (that is, about one-third of all family law cases in the courts) occur in this way. These cases are focused heavily on the protection function of the system (since this is such a major part of the District Court's work in family law) and to a lesser extent on the limited aspects of the separation function which are available in the District Court. Cases of this kind have a relatively fleeting contact with the family law system — they are likely to have only a brief appearance in court, to have no prior legal consultation or advice and no contact with other legally-related support services (since the latter do not exist to any great extent). Legally represented cases, by contrast, are more likely to be oriented to the separation function and to the Circuit Court. They are also more likely to involve extended intensive involvement with the family law system — the median duration of separation cases which require adjudication in the Circuit Court is two and a half years, compared to three to six weeks for a barring case in the District Court. However, one factor which tends to shorten and simplify the otherwise complicated nature of legally represented cases is the high rate of out-of-court settlements, sometimes helped by family mediation. It takes a median period of one year to arrive at a legal separation agreement, somewhat longer if the parties take that agreement to court to have it converted into a judicial separation order by consent. The majority of legally represented separation cases do not go to adjudication.

The dualism between legally represented and legally unrepresented cases is diluted and complicated to some extent by the existence of a significant sub-division among legally represented cases. This sub-division arises between cases involving private solicitors and those involving legal aid solicitors. Cases represented by private solicitors conform quite markedly to the general character of legally represented cases — a focus on separation rather than protection and on the Circuit Court rather than the District Court. Legal aid cases form a transitional category between privately represented cases and those cases which have no legal representation at all. Some are broadly similar to the general run of legally represented cases, in that they are focused on legal separation and on the Circuit Court — though if geared to separation, they are less likely to use family mediation and less likely to arrive at an agreed settlement than privately represented cases. Other legal aid cases, however, have more in common with legally unrepresented cases — they are more likely to be oriented to the District Court, to focus on the protection function or on isolated aspects of the separation function, and to take a shorter time to complete. And of course, legal aid cases are more likely to be concentrated among the economically insecure. Cases represented by legal aid solicitors, therefore, reduce the sharpness of the dualism between legally represented and legally unrepresented cases. They do not eliminate the dualism entirely but mean that we should speak of a continuum between two extremes rather than a sharp division.

The large numbers of legally unrepresented cases in the family law system is also notable for the substantial role it gives District Court clerks in processing family law cases. Though, strictly speaking, their function in the court system is purely administrative, District Court clerks in practice often play an important role in advising and guiding clients for whom they are the first stop in approaching the family law system.

Dualism of Economic Status

The economic profile of solicitors' family law clients is dominated by two main clusters — the two-earner couple living in owner-occupied housing on the one hand, and the welfare-dependent couple with a higher than average likelihood of living in rented accommodation (local authority or private) on the other. It thus tends to polarise around two levels of advantage and disadvantage as far as employment status and housing is concerned. What we often think of as the middle-ground, standard family type — the bread-winner husband and stay-at-home wife — is considerably under-represented among solicitors' clients.

The dualism of economic status, however, is *not* a social class dualism. Solicitors' family law clients, particularly those who receive legal aid, are disproportionately drawn from the lower non-manual and medium-sized farming class. The working classes as a whole are under-represented, and are as likely to rely on private solicitors as on legal aid. The professional classes are somewhat over-represented and a minority of these are likely to rely on legal aid. Thus, the kind of economic stress which is likely to qualify clients to receive legal aid is spread over the whole range of social classes and is especially present in the lower middle class. The cross-class character of such economic stress indicates that it may be particularly prevalent among families in all social classes which experience marital breakdown — economic difficulties may be part cause of breakdown and may be part consequence, particularly for women.

The economic dualism just described has been identified only in connection with solicitors' clients. We lacked the necessary information to examine the economic profile of legally un-represented cases which make up such a large proportion of family law business in the District Court. It is possible that the working classes figure more prominently in that category of family law case, thus accounting to some extent for their relatively weak presence among solicitors' clients.

As with the other dualisms we have looked at, the dualism of economic status is marked by a substantial incidence of ex-ceptions and transitional cases which form a bridge between the two dominant clusters. The breadwinner husband plus stay-at-home wife may be statistically under-represented among family law cases but they do still occur in significant numbers. The welfare-dependent cluster of cases is slightly more likely to have a minority of unmarried couples and the two-earner cluster is slightly more likely to have no dependent children. Both clusters, however, have a majority of married couples, aged in their late 30s or 40s, who have been married for at least 10 years and who have dependent children.

Dualism of Outcomes

A final variation to note in family law cases concerns the ma-terial aspect of their legal outcomes. Maintenance arrange-ments and property settlements, particularly concerning the family home, are a standard part of the resolution of disputes for the better-off, separation-oriented family law cases. How-ever, they are a great deal less significant for the less well off. A majority of legal aid cases, for example, include neither maintenance arrangements nor property settlements in the outcome of cases. This reflects the high proportion of welfare-dependent, non-property owning couples among legal aid cases.

As far the living arrangements of children are concerned, however, there was no observable difference across social groups: children generally ended up living with their mothers.

A Two-tier System?

In drawing together the dualisms in family law into a single picture, we do not want to provide an excessively neat characterisation of the divisions in the system. There are many exceptions and transitional cases which do not fit with the distinctions we have made or which blur the boundaries between them. Nevertheless, there is enough evidence to suggest that each one of the dualisms on its own has some validity. More interestingly, there are indications that the individual dualisms tend to overlay each other and so tend towards a two-tier structure in the overall system. The lower tier is dominated by cases which are centred on protection against domestic violence, or, to a lesser extent, on discrete aspects of martial separation such as maintenance and child access, which take place in the District Court, which are legally unrepresented or represented by legal aid solicitors, and which have a heavy concentration of less well-off couples, particularly in that one or both partners may be dependent on social welfare and are much less likely to be in owner-occupied housing than the population at large. The upper tier is dominated by cases which are concerned with fully-fledged legal separation, which are focused on the Circuit Court or else try to arrive at separation agreements without going to court, which are represented by private solicitors or, to a lesser extent, by legal aid solicitors, and which have an over-representation of better-off couples, particularly in that both partners may have paid jobs.

As a general summation of the system, this two-tier structure is even more of a simplification of reality than the individual dichotomies which make it up. However, it has enough substance to remind us that family law has more to it than legal separation. At the beginning of this study, we noted that the practice of family law in most countries tends to be centred around a single dominant focus — divorce — and to that extent is usually thought of as having a fairly unitary character. In Ireland, we often think of legal separation as the functional parallel to divorce, similar to divorce in most respects except that the right to remarry is absent. We also tend to think of a certain set of legal procedures and services associated with separation — solicitors and family mediation, tortuous proceedings under the Judicial Separation and Family Law Reform Act, 1989, disputes about maintenance, child access and child custody, the disposition of the family home — as part of the package which defines what family law is about.

Now we see that this focus reflects only one segment of family law — the upper tier as we have just described it. The lower tier represents an equally large and equally important segment of the system. This tier is less visible, less well recognised and the cases which make it up, though numerous, have less intensive involvement with the legal system. The legal services and procedures which are so prominent in this tier — the District Court and District Court clerks, lack of legal representation, quick proceedings and blunt legal outcomes, and a less frequent concern with either property settlements or maintenance arrangements — also belong to a somewhat different world than those of the upper tier. At the same time, the family problems which give rise to cases within this tier are no less severe, and often are far more severe, than those of the upper tier. This is so particularly given the prominence of domestic violence as the central feature of so many of these cases.

Issues and Implications

This study has not been designed to yield prescriptions for family law reform. Nevertheless, certain issues emerge from the study which need to be addressed if family law is to develop an adequate response to family conflict and breakdown. Most of these issues relate in one way or another to what we have described as a strong tendency towards dualism in the family law system. They arise in particular from the relative neglect of what we characterised as the lower tier of the system in reflection and debate about family law reform in Ireland. Here we can simply summarise what some of those key issues are.

Domestic Violence and Family Law

The first such issue is the scale of domestic violence which is revealed by the numbers of protection and barring cases in the system at present, particularly in the lower tier. Domestic violence has long been acknowledged as a social problem in

Ireland and the system of family law has been mobilised to provide a response. Since the early 1980s, domestic violence seems to have been the single most common precipitating factor behind family law cases appearing before the Irish courts. Certain voluntary bodies and women's groups have taken a keen interest in this subject and the recent Domestic Violence Bill shows that policy makers have been conscious of it as well.[1]

However, beyond that, there has been little general recognition of the centrality of domestic violence in patterns of marital breakdown. There has been scarcely any systematic investigation into the practical operation of the Family Law (Protection of Spouses and Children) Act, 1981, nor indeed any recognition of the centrality of this statute to the practical operation of family law in Ireland. Even the basic policy-making resource represented by court statistics on the subject is highly inadequate. Those statistics give us no information on the family and social circumstances of typical barring cases, nor do they provide such basic monitoring data as the number of new barring cases each year or the proportion of barring applicants who make repeated returns to the courts for renewals of barring orders. Beyond that, we have no systematic information on the extent to which protection and barring orders are enforced, their effectiveness in preventing further domestic violence or the extent to which barred husbands depart the family home and never return.

The present study has not been able to address these questions in any detail. But it has been able to point out how important they are and how necessary it is that they be taken account of in public debate about marital breakdown and family law reform. Particular attention needs to be paid to one of the most striking features of the present legal response to domestic violence — its blunt and abrupt nature. Applications for barring orders can reflect the most traumatic forms of family disruption and are likely to have a serious impact on the family if granted (and perhaps an equally serious impact if they

----

[1] The recently-published work by Browne and Connolly (1995) came to hand too late to be taken into account in the present study.

lapse or are refused). Yet they can pass through the system in a short time, with the minimum of attention, quite often without legal advice or representation and with no systematic follow-up.

This despatch, in one sense, is a virtue of the present system. It means that applicant spouses get a quicker response than is normal in family law cases and have to cope with less by way of legal formalities, expense and delays, along with the stress these give rise to. It would not be uncommon for a barring application to be lodged, heard and granted in the District Court within the space of three or four weeks, in contrast with delays of months or even years for separation proceedings in the Circuit Court. It could also cost almost nothing in money terms: in contrast with the Circuit Court, the proceedings might be issued without charge by the District Court clerk and heard without legal representation on either the applicant's or respondent's part. Since barring applications are civil rather than criminal procedures, and since District Court procedures in general are less strict and formal than Circuit Court procedures, the scrutiny of the issues and the standard of evidence in barring cases would be likely to be less stringent that in separation cases in the Circuit Court.

On the other hand, the quick, brief handling of barring applications means that some of the most damaged, dysfunctional families which appear before the courts are offered only the crudest of legal remedies and get no additional support or follow-up. The remedy itself is one of the most drastic available to family law — immediate, forcible ejection of the offending spouse from the family home. It is by nature an emergency response, and as such is necessary, but it is hardly sufficient as a long-term solution. The context in which it is offered is also questionable. Most District Court judges have no specialised training in family law, much less in the psychology of family violence. The District Court has little or no access to professional social services support, either as a resource for informed judgement or as an extension of the remedies available to clients (neither, should it be said, has the Circuit Court, though the level of trauma in Circuit Court cases may be less and the private resources of clients for dealing with that trauma may be greater than in the typical District Court case).

The family law system thus offers no help to families in repairing the damage they have suffered from domestic violence and no recognition that the damage will still be there even after the offending spouse has been removed. The recently proposed Domestic Violence Bill concentrates on improving the emergency response — bringing additional forms of domestic violence within the ambit of the protective legislation and strengthening the enforcement procedures. Necessary though such improvements may be, they do not go beyond the immediate emergency to address the longer-term issues. In that light, the recommendations by the Law Reform Commission concerning the broader reform of the system of family courts become important, particularly the recommendation that family social services be attached to the family courts to deal with the social circumstances of family law cases (Law Reform Commission, 1994). Nowhere do such support services seem more necessary than in cases of domestic violence.

Domestic Violence and Legal Separation

A further striking feature of the present system is the degree to which its two major functions — protection against domestic violence and legal separation — operate in isolation from each other. As noted earlier, some family law cases embrace both functions but most do not. One way of accounting for this division is to argue that it is a reflection of the objectively different nature of the two kinds of family cases. The acts which give rise to barring orders — the exercise of violence against family members — are distinctive in that they might equally well give rise to criminal cases of assault. It could be said, in fact, that barring procedures have the effect of bringing what in effect are criminal acts within the ambit of family-related civil proceedings. The conflicts giving rise to separation procedures, by contrast, have a more unambiguously civil character — they centre on disputes between persons rather than on what might be regarded as breaches of the criminal law.

However, while these objective differences in case types are there, it is also highly likely that the gulf between the protection and separation functions of the family law system is as much a product of the family law system as of the nature of family conflicts. The key issue here is that, as already noted, the protection function is quick, cheap and accessible while the separation function is none of these things. The protection function can also be quite potent and yield considerable separation-like effects. Most basically, barring orders have the effect of ejecting the respondent spouse from the family home, thereby implicitly transferring right of residence in the family home and custody of children to the applicant spouse, at least for the duration of the barring order. If the applicant felt it necessary, she could have these outcomes reinforced by applying for orders dealing with custody of children and the father's rights of access to them in conjunction with the barring application. If she were dependent on her husband for financial support, she could also add in an application for maintenance. In short, the granting of a barring order in the District Court, especially when maintenance and guardianship orders are added on, can have a range of practical outcomes similar to those available in separation proceedings in the Circuit Court.

In principle, Circuit Court proceedings under the 1989 Act could serve the protection function, since emergency barring orders can be obtained quite quickly as part of separation proceedings in the Circuit Court. One might also expect that victims of domestic violence, once they had taken the initiative of seeking a barring order, would often want to go the whole way and get a full legal separation. In practice, the majority of victims of domestic violence who have recourse to family law do not take that route. This may be so partly because they do not want to — protection may be all that they require and full legal separation may be irrelevant to their needs. This might be so especially for the non-property-owning, welfare-dependent families who make heavy use of the barring remedy. It is also possible, however, that many such clients would seek legal separation if it were sufficiently accessible, and that the present division between protection and separation cases is really due to the cumbersome operation of the separation function within the family law system. The difficulty in mounting a separation case is likely to be especially severe if the level of co-operation between spouses is low, as one might expect to be the case in marriages with a history of violence.

Full and Partial Legal Separation

The division between the protection and separation functions of the family law system is paralleled on a smaller scale within the separation function itself. Here the division is between full legal separation (as available from the Circuit Court or by out-of-court agreement) and partial separation in the District Court (by way of discrete orders for maintenance, custody or access, usually without any more comprehensive separation follow-up). The factors leading to this division are likely to be broadly similar to those which create the larger division between protection and separation — a combination of client need and procedural characteristics of the different legal remedies. Clients who obtain what we call partial separation may not want anything more. Alternatively, they might prefer a more comprehensive settlement but are deterred from seeking it by the nature of the proceedings they would have to undertake. In narrow legal terms, the Judicial Separation and Family Law Reform Act, 1989 offers the most powerful and flexible means of providing comprehensive separation settlements available in the Irish family law system. In practice, the procedural and administrative infrastructure which delivers that remedy is anything but smooth and efficient. As a result, the 1989 Act plays a smaller role in legal separation than its legal character would warrant.

Agreed and Adjudicated Separation

Separation cases that are actually adjudicated in the Circuit Court form a minority of fully-fledged separation cases (and an even smaller minority of full and partial separation cases combined). Separation agreements arrived at without going to court and separation orders by consent (which go to court but without a requirement for adjudication) together amount to a larger proportion of full separation settlements.

It is often thought desirable that marital separation be settled by agreement rather than by adjudication, so that this might be thought of as a positive feature of the system. However, consensual settlement has an unambiguously positive character only when it is chosen as an option, not imposed by the lack of an alternative. In principle, agreed settlements in marital separation should be arrived at "in the shadow of the law" — the courts should be available to step in where the parties cannot agree and to provide a check on agreements that are made to ensure that they are equitable and just to both sides and their children. In Ireland at present, it appears that the shadow of the law, in this sense, is often faint and remote. Court adjudication is often difficult to obtain — though paradoxically, where it is provided it is often criticised for being too directive and heavy-handed (Law Reform Commission, 1994, p. 136). In any event, the weaker parties in marital separation cases may well make do with settlements which are unfair to them but which they have to accept simply because they lack the strength, endurance or financial resources necessary to fight through to a court hearing.

We cannot say to what extent this actually happens, but it is possible that the present system does not provide adequate safeguards against unjust consensual settlements. This may be so in part because the Circuit Court is not adequately equipped to provide good judgements in the cases it does deal with (a view strongly advanced by the Law Reform Commission, 1994). But is also likely to arise because of barriers to access to the adjudicating function of the Circuit Court in family law cases. These barriers arise partly in the form of cost — Circuit Court proceedings requires the services of solicitors and barristers and so require a certain level of financial resources. While legal aid services go some of the way towards over-coming these cost barriers for less well-off couples, it is not clear that they are available widely enough and quickly enough to meet needs of all those who require them.

Cost is not the only barrier, however. The Circuit Court is unable to cope adequately with the present volume of family law business, so that large backlogs and lengthy delays in processing cases are common. In addition, the nature of the proceedings are such that they usually take a long time to complete. It may be true that justice and completeness in family law cases is often best served by a slow, thorough approach. It may also be true that no procedures can be devised to simplify or shorten bitterly contested cases where the partners are willing to fight to the finish. But, within those constraints, it is important to ensure that legal procedures and the adequacy of court facilities should not form an unnecessary impediment to court adjudication in family law cases.

This is not to say that a more adequate, accessible and client-friendly system would result in a higher proportion of cases going to adjudication. The opposite might well be true, and might well be achieved if a more widely available system of family advice and mediation were put in place. It means rather that adjudication would be more widely and immediately available *in the background*, as an option to be drawn upon if necessary. Separation agreements might be arrived at more quickly and more fairly if such an option were genuinely available. The Circuit Court can best perform its role as referee in marital separation cases not necessarily by getting involved in every case but by being closer to hand so that both sides know that it can be called in if either of them begin to play fast and loose with the rules of fair play. Current patterns suggest that it is not playing that role adequately at present.

Integration of the Family Law System

The dualisms we have noted in the family law system give rise to the question as to whether a more integrated, streamlined structure would be more desirable. The Law Reform Commission has raised this question in detail, pointing to the fragmented nature of family law jurisdiction and the complexity in legal documents and procedures which is partly caused by this fragmentation. Its consultation paper on the family courts has provisionally proposed a specialised, uniform system of eight to ten regional family courts, organised as a specialised division of the Circuit Court (Law Reform Commission, 1994). It recommends also that the facilities of the new family court be vastly improved by way of better premises and better trained specialist judges and also by the addition of family advice centres to be attached to the new regional family courts. Furthermore, it recommends closer integration between the court and various family services, especially in regard to counselling and mediation.

It is beyond our competence to comment in any detail on these recommendations, other than to say that they reflect a well-founded diagnosis of the defects in the present Circuit Court system. However, there is one aspect of the recommendations we would comment on — their tendency to focus on what we have called the upper tier of the system and to pay relatively little attention to the lower tier. Most of the Commission's proposals focus on the Circuit Court and High Court levels of the system. The proposed new family courts would, in effect, take over and enhance the current roles of the Circuit Court and the High Court in family law. The District Court, the Commission suggests, should retain something like its present role — dealing with emergency protection cases and with certain individual aspects of separation such as maintenance, custody and access. Otherwise, it pays little attention to the District Court, and thereby seems to imply that the present operation of the District Court in family law cases is unproblematic, or is somehow of secondary significance in the family law system.

We would not necessarily want to reverse this order of priority but we would suggest that any reform of the system should take a genuinely integrated approach. This means that the role and function of the District Court in family law should be taken fully into account. At present, the District Court, despite the limited nature of its powers and facilities, is the more widely used of the two main court levels in the family law system. Its principal virtue seems to be its accessibility. It responds to a need among family law clients for ease, speed and simplicity of response, or at least does so more effectively than the Circuit Court. Paradoxically, it is able to respond in that way precisely because of its narrow, disaggregated powers: it can deal with individual aspects of family conflict separately, without probing too far into the broader circumstances of the family or without being obliged to take a comprehensive view. The remedies which result may have a rough and ready, piecemeal character, but at least they are there to be obtained, in contrast to the more elaborate but more inaccessible remedies of the Circuit Court.

In any reform of the system, the problems and defects which arise at the District Court level should be given as much as, if not more, attention than those arising at the Circuit Court level. The factors which underlie the present distribution of the family law caseload between the District Court and the Circuit Court should be fully understood, the desirability of altering that balance should be explored, and the mechanisms by which any such alteration are to be achieved should be thought out. It is particularly important that the role of the District Court in dealing with domestic violence be brought into the centre of the picture and assessed, not in terms of emergency response but also in terms of longer-term remedies for families affected by domestic violence.

Implications for Divorce Legislation

The present study has not been concerned with the question of divorce and cannot draw any conclusions on whether the introduction of divorce is desirable or not. However, some implications do arise concerning the likely impact of divorce legislation on the present family law system. One is that the present court system is not adequately resourced to deal with extra family law business, and so would have difficulty coping with the new stream of demands which the introduction of divorce would give rise to. This is especially so since divorce would be likely to be a Circuit Court rather than a District Court function: at present, it is the Circuit Court system which is particularly overburdened by the present level of family law business.

In addition, one of the common concerns of those who are willing to contemplate the legalisation of divorce is that divorce should not be "easy" — there should be no possibility of a "quickie divorce". If the present operation of the family law system is anything to go by, this concern is misplaced. There is nothing quick or easy about present Circuit Court procedures for legal separation, especially in cases which require adjudication. There are no grounds for thinking that divorce proceedings would be any different, especially if divorce could be granted to applicants only after legal separation had been obtained.

We can be more precise about this point if we distinguish two different aspects of the easiness or otherwise of separation or divorce proceedings. One aspect relates to the stringency (or lack of it) in the legal grounds on which divorce or separation may be obtained, the other relates to the accessibility and efficiency of divorce or separation proceedings in the courts. At present, legal separation in Ireland is reasonably "easy" from the former of these points of view but quite difficult from the latter. "Marital breakdown" for at least a year is the most common ground for judicial separation. This ground can be interpreted quite liberally, and in that sense separation is easy. However, no rush to the courts to seek judicial separation has occurred as a result. Although the number of separation cases in the Circuit Court has increased sharply since the introduction of the 1989 Act, the increase occurred from a low base and the present total still accounts for only a portion of all family law cases. In particular, the numbers of cases actually processed under the 1989 Act (as opposed to the number of applications made) is still relatively small.

If the divorce option were introduced, it might be little utilised if it were to be as difficult to access and process as the present system of adjudicated separation. This aspect of the "easiness" of divorce might well be a more important determinant of its practical impact than the formal legal grounds on which divorce might be obtained.

One final point arises about the legalisation of divorce. As already mentioned, one common view is that, if divorce were to be legalised, it should be made conditional on a certain period of separation. If that approach were to be adopted, some thought would need to be given as to how separation should be defined. One possibility is that separation be defined in terms of residential (or *de facto*) separation. In that case the question of proof of separation could become central. What evidence would applicants for divorce be required to give to substantiate the claim that they had ceased to live with their partners on a particular date? The difficulty here is that if a long period of separation were required as a precondition of divorce, couples might have an incentive to collude in back-dating their date of separation in order to achieve the qualifying period more quickly (it is possible to envisage that friends or family members might assist in such collusion by giving evidence of having provided accommodation to one of the spouses from a particular date). If such collusion became widespread, the prescribed separation criterion, however justified in principle, might become difficult to sustain in practice.

An alternative approach would be to define separation by reference to some legally marked transition, for example, the issuing of a barring or maintenance order, the formalising of a separation agreement or the issuing of a judicial separation order. These would have the virtue of being formally registered (or, in the case of a separation agreement, of being capable of being so), so that their dating could be easily verified. However, they would have a less than uniform relationship with the dating of *de facto* separation. The issuing of a barring order, for example, might give rise to and thus coincide with *de facto* separation, while a judicial separation order might not be obtained until years after a *de facto* separation had occurred. Here too, anomalies could arise in the application of the separation criterion which might make it difficult to sustain in practice.

Children and Family Law

As we said in the introduction to this study, we originally had the intention of focusing in some detail on the place of children in the family law system, largely in response to the widespread concern about the impact of marital breakdown on children. We could not hope to assess how marital breakdown affects children, but it did seem feasible and useful to ask how the legal response to marital breakdown reflects and handles children's interests.

In the event, our study yielded little information on this question. It did provide some data on the proportions of family law cases which involve children, on the extent to which children were a focus of conflict in those cases and on the residence outcomes for children after separation took place. Otherwise, however, children were shadowy presences in our data sources. Official statistics on family law cases in the courts make no reference to children, other than to report the gross number of guardianship applications in the District Court (the principal proceedings directly related to children in the family law system). Even at that, these data do not provide breakdowns by type of application (access, custody or guardianship in the narrower sense), they give no information on the number or ages of children at issue, nor do they report the number or substance of the orders granted. Likewise, official data on applications for judicial separation give no information on the numbers of such applications which include ancillary applications for custody, access or maintenance orders regarding children.

In the data on the solicitors' case-file sample, our main information source, children are secondary figures. This reflects the nature of legal representation in the system as presently constituted. The solicitor's job is to represent his or her client — the parent. The question of representation for the child does not arise and the child's point of view is not directly expressed in the processing of cases. It is scarcely surprising, therefore, that the solicitor's perspective on family law cases is focused on the adults rather than the children involved.

The Judicial Separation and Family Law Reform Act, 1989 requires the Circuit Court to ensure that adequate provision is made for children before a judicial separation is granted. However, it institutes no mechanism through which the child's requirements or the child's preferences can be directly expressed to the court. Judges may choose to interview children in chambers, separately from the litigating parents. Sometimes, it appears, they do so, though we have no information on how often that happens. It is also possible for the court to request child profiles from social workers or psychologists. Again, we lack information on how widely expert information of that type is used, though our impression is that it is the exception rather than the rule. Indeed, solicitors often complain of how difficult it is to secure profiles or assessments of this type from the social services, even in traumatic cases where they might be a basic requirement. In general, it seems that the child's voice is heard only through the parent's, sometimes in the context of a bitter conflict between the father and the mother as to what is best for the child.

In any event, only a minority of family law cases go through the full judicial separation procedures where court oversight of the provisions for children is a requirement. More usually, family law cases which go to court do so in the District Court, where there is no legal requirement that the child's interests be systematically taken into account. Many other cases are settled by agreement, without going to court. The provisions for children in these agreements are likely to be influenced in a general way by the legal context provided by various statutes, especially the 1989 Act. Again however, this influence is indirect and has an unknown impact on the way children's interests are handled.

The absence of children from our study, therefore, is a reflection of their marginal position in the family law system. It is a commonplace of public debate to express concern about the impact on children of marital breakdown and divorce. It is less common for policy makers to ask if the present legal response to family conflict takes adequate account of children's interests, or uses all the resources it might to reflect and respond to the child's viewpoint. Our impression is that it does not do these things. Our even stronger impression is that there has been little systematic investigation to find out whether this is so, or how general expressions of concern about children's welfare might be translated into practical improvements in the processing of family law cases.

Gender and Family Law

In Ireland, the law on marital breakdown generally is a woman's resource rather than a man's resource. This is evidenced especially in the very large proportion of cases which are initiated by women. Applications concerned with questions of guardianship and access to children are the only type of proceeding in which men are marginally more likely than women to take the initiative (particularly where the man is not married to the mother of his children). These account for only a small proportion of the total of cases. In addition, certain important statutes, especially the Family Law (Protection of

Spouses and Children) Act, 1981 and the Judicial Separation and Family Law Reform Act, 1989 give extensive powers to the courts to weight judgements in the woman's favour.

In principle, therefore, family law could have a major part to play in redressing the imbalances of power and advantage between women and men which exist within family life, particularly in situations of family conflict. In practice, certain parts of the family law system appear to fail in achieving that end — see, for example, Ward's (1990) account of the inadequacy of the system of maintenance support from the recipient's point of view. The information available to us in the present study does not allow us to judge how widespread such failures are, or which areas of the law are inadequate from this point of view. In general, the study suggests that the way the law is implemented is as important as the content of the law in shaping its practical effect. We therefore need to know not only what happens in court but also within the family law system more generally. We also need to know what happens afterwards as men and women adjust to whatever outcome the system offers them. It is by reference to these long-term consequences rather than to the immediate legal outcomes that the question of gender balance in the family law system can be judged.

METHODS AND DATA

Two data collection exercises were carried out for the present study. The first and larger of the two exercises consisted of a survey of 87 solicitors which collected information on 510 of their family law case files. The second and smaller exercise was a more restricted survey of 130 family law cases in the family court (Dolphin House) in the Dublin Metropolitan District, with information provided by Court Registrars. In this appendix we will describe in turn how each of these sources was compiled.

Solicitors' Case-Files Sample

The survey of solicitors' case-files was designed to gather information on a national representative sample of solicitors' family law cases, including both private and legal aid solicitors. This required first that we identify and contact a representative sample of solicitors who practised family law. Adequate sampling of such solicitors was made difficult by the lack of any national listing of solicitors who practise family law and by the absence of information on how the total family law case load they handle is distributed (for example, by region or by type of firm). To overcome this difficulty, we initially considered screening by telephone interview a large national random sample of solicitors so as to identify those who practised family law and to get information on the size and structure of their family law caseload. However, we soon abandoned that approach as too cumbersome and expensive and decided instead to design the sample on the basis of indirect information and informed guesses about how the family law case load was distributed among solicitors.

Private and Legal Aid Solicitors

The first concern was the distribution of the sample between private solicitors and solicitors employed in Law Centres by the Legal Aid Board. This was a crucial question from a research point of view since we had to assume that there would be substantial differences in the social dimensions of family law cases between private and legal aid family law practices. However, while Legal Aid Board statistics could tell us the size of the family law case-load carried by the Board's solicitors, we had no corresponding data about private family law practice. In consequence, we had no fully reliable basis on which to allocate the sample between private and legal aid solicitors. In the absence of any better guide, we had to rely on rough guesses on this question, principally as supplied by staff of the Legal Aid Board. On the basis of such informed guesswork, we initially allocated two-thirds of the sample to private solicitors and the remaining one-third to legal aid solicitors. In the event, we slightly overshot our target for private solicitors because of a lower than expected refusal/non-participation rate among them. As a result, private family law cases amounted to 70 per cent of the final sample.

Given the lack of independent checks on the adequacy of this distribution, we have to accept that it could be biased one way or the other. For that reason, in the body of the present report we have generally presented case-file data from private and legal aid solicitors separately, as if the two bodies of data were drawn from separate samples for separate populations. For most variables, we have more confidence in the two samples separately than we have in the aggregate sample. However, on a number of variables there was no significant difference between the two constituent samples and in those instances we sometimes present data on the aggregate sample without making the private/legal aid distinction.

Area Distribution of Sample

The second concern in sampling cases was the distribution of the sample by area. This was complicated by the fact that the area distribution of family law proceedings in the Circuit

Court differed from that in the District Court. Thus, for example, Dublin accounted for nearly half of all family law applications in the District Court but only 14 per cent of judicial separation cases in the Circuit Court (see Chapter Two above). Furthermore, no information was available on the area distribution of family law cases which were settled by solicitors without going to court. We therefore lacked a single comprehensive measure of the area distribution of family law cases.

Our solution for sampling purposes was to allocate the sample of private solicitors according to an approximate compromise between the area distribution of District Court and Circuit Court family law business. This resulted in an allocation of 40 per cent of the sample to Dublin, 15 per cent to Cork city and county, and the remaining 45 per cent to the rest of the country.

To simplify data collection, we then clustered the sample outside of Dublin and Cork in five major areas — the Limerick city–Ennis corridor; Mayo–Galway (centred on the Castlebar area); the Waterford city–Dungarvan area; north Kildare–south Meath, reaching into the Dundalk area; and north Offaly (see Table A.1). Each of these areas contains a Law Centre (as local offices of the Legal Aid Board are called) along with large numbers of private solicitors. All the solicitors we eventually selected were based in towns, large or small. However, their clients were drawn from larger hinterlands, so that the sample of clients is more widely dispersed than the sample of solicitors. The area distribution of the sample does not have the same importance from a research point of view as its distribution between private and legal aid solicitors. This is so partly because the area distribution of the sample seems to be reasonable in the light of available data and partly because, from subsequent analysis of the data, area appears not to be a major determinant of characteristics of family law cases. In consequence, even if the area distribution were somewhat inaccurate, it would be unlikely to introduce serious biases into the sample.

Table A.1: Sample of Family Law Case-Files by Area and by Type of Legal Representation

Area	Type of Legal Representation					Total Cases
	Private Solicitors		*Legal Aid Solicitors*			
	No of Solicitors	*No of Cases*	*Law Centres*	*No of Solicitors*	*No of Cases*	
Dublin city and county	27	147	Tallaght	3	15	
			Clondalkin	2	15	207
			Finglas	1	15	
			Gardiner St	3	15	
Cork city	7	42	North Mall	1	9	77
Cork county	2	12	South Mall	3	14	
Limerick – Clare	7	42	Limerick	3	20	62
Mayo-Galway	6	34	Castlebar	2	12	46
Waterford – Dungarvan area	6	36	Waterford	3	18	54
Offaly	3	16	Athlone	1	10	26
Meath – Kildare	5	28	Dundalk	2	10	38
Total	63	357		24	153	510

Selecting Solicitors

Within the areas identified, private solicitors were selected for inclusion in the sample with the help of the Family Law Committee of the Law Society. The aim was to contact solicitors who were known to have or were likely to have some involvement in family law practice. The members of the Family Law Committee did not always have enough local knowledge to identify such solicitors accurately but they did help to reduce the incidence in the sample of solicitors who had no involvement whatever with family law. In cases where the solicitor contacted did not practice family law, we asked if any other solicitor in the firm did and took that alternative as a substitute where it was available. If no solicitor in the firm practised family law, no further requests for substitutes were made.

Because of the non-randomness of the sampling procedure, we cannot be sure if the resulting sample of solicitors is fully representative of all private solicitors who practice family law. However, we feel that it is sufficiently varied and dispersed to ensure that no major distortions occur in the subsequent sample of private family law cases, particularly since, within family law practice, we could see no evidence of systematic links between solicitor characteristics and characteristics of family law cases.

In the case of legal aid solicitors, we first selected ten Law Centres — four in Dublin, two in Cork and one in each of the other five areas in the study. We then allocated the sample of legal aid cases across these ten centres in such a way as to achieve the area distribution outlined earlier. As the bulk of cases dealt with by Law Centres are family law cases (Legal Aid Board, 1993), we did not attempt to sample individual solicitors from these Law Centres in advance. Rather, we left it to the solicitor-in-charge in each Centre to arrange how many and which solicitors in the Centre would participate in the study.

Selecting Cases

The normal quota of cases which we wished to include from each solicitor was six. In the case of legal aid solicitors, the quota was sometimes above that, since the quota was determined by reference to the Law Centre rather than to the solicitors within each Centre. Interviewers were instructed not to include cases which consisted of consultation only (that is, where the solicitor provided the client only with information or advice and did not undertake to begin any action).

Only those cases which were current at time of interview or had been concluded within the previous six months were to be included. (In the event, 54 per cent of cases included in the sample were current, while 46 per cent concluded, most of them within one to two months of survey date).

Cases were selected under the interviewer's direction at point of interview. The normal method used to randomise the selection was for the interviewer to take a series of letters of the alphabet (for example, *k, l, m, n, o, p*) and to ask the solicitor to select the first family law case under each of those letters in his or her filing system. This process continued until the desired quota of cases was reached. If the solicitor did not keep files in alphabetical order, some other procedure was used — for example, picking files at random from a pile or from an array of shelves. One important concern was not to allow the solicitor to decide which cases should be picked (for example, so as to pick "good ones" or "easy ones").

In order to protect the confidentiality of files, interviewers were instructed not to ask the client's name or any other identifying information, and not to ask to see any of the documentation connected with the file.

Dublin Metropolitan District Court Sample

The second original data source used in the study consisted of information collected on 132 family law cases in the Dublin Metropolitan District (DMD) Court. The purpose of this data source was to supplement the solicitors' case file sample, principally by providing a means to estimate the proportion of family law cases in the District Court which were taken without legal representation and by gathering some basic information on such cases. The sample was confined to the DMD because of lack of the resources necessary to extend it to other parts of the country. It is worth recalling, however, that the DMD Court accounts for approximately half of the national family law case load at District Court level.

As the documentary records held by the District Court on the cases it processes is very limited, and as access to clients and court hearings by outside researchers is restricted by the *in camera* rules which apply to family law cases, indirect methods of data collection had to be used in this instance. Following discussion with the administrative staff in the DMD Court, it was arranged that the information would be collected through the Court Registrars. Where their work-loads allowed it, the Court Registrars undertook to complete a short information form on the family law cases appearing before the

DMD Court on a random selection of days between early November 1994 and the end of January 1995. The initial target sample was 200 cases. In the event, because of pressure of work on court registrars, it proved possible to achieve a sample of only 132 cases.

The range of information sought on these cases was much narrower than that gathered in the solicitor's case-file sample. It related, first, to the social circumstances of litigants (age, marital status and number and ages of children of the applicant, type of housing tenure, and the employment status and occupation of both the applicant and the respondent) and secondly, to certain legal aspects of the case (the nature and outcome of the proceedings, whether or not the applicant or respondent had legal representation and whether or not the respondent was in court on the day of the hearing). In most cases, this information was drawn from advance documents presented for the court hearing or from details which were evident or emerged during the hearing itself.

The information from these sources did not always cover all of the required items, particularly regarding the social circumstances of litigants. The items on housing tenure, employment status and occupation in particular were often not required for the processing of the case and so did not emerge before or during the court hearing. In those instances, since the pressure on time and resources did not allow for use of any additional information sources (such as interviews with applicants or respondents), these items had to be left blank. In other instances, particularly regarding occupation, the available information was patchy and was of limited use for analysis. Those items which did relate more directly to the substance of the case, such as the marital status of the applicant, the nature and outcome of the proceedings and whether or not the applicant or respondent were legally represented in court, were usually available and were recorded in the great majority of cases in the sample.

The DMD Court sample was thus small, confined to the Dublin District and provided only limited information. Nevertheless, because of the lack of alternative data sources on District Court family law cases, it provided a useful additional information source for this study.

APPENDIX II

SOLICITOR'S CASE-FILE DATA RECORDING FORM

28 November 1994

Family Disruption, Children and the Law:

Solicitor's Case-File Data Recording Form

Note:
- *Select from case files which have been open at some time in the past 6 months (i.e. which are still active or which were finalised within the past 6 months)*
- *Do not include cases which consisted of once-off consultation only*

Solicitor Code ☐☐☐   Case-file code ☐☐
Solicitors file reference_____ Intvr. name_____

SECTION I. CONTACT WITH CLIENT

1. When did you/your firm take on the present case (refer only to present family law proceedings with client: discount any prior dealings on other matters).

        Month_____/Year 19_____

2. When did you last speak to your client about the case:

        Month_____/Year 19_____

SECTION II: PERSONAL DETAILS OF CLIENT

3. Sex: Male ☐1   Female ☐2

4. Year of Birth: 19____ or age group:
      15-19☐1   20-24☐2   25-29☐3   30-34☐4
      35-39☐5   40-44☐6   45-49☐7   50-54☐8
      55-59☐9   60-64☐10   65 + ☐11

5. (a) What is or was the nature of the clients relationship with the principal other party in this case?

Marriage	❏1
Extended cohabitation (more than 1 yr)	❏2
Occasional or short cohabitation (less than 1 yr)	❏3
Non-cohabiting relationship/affair	❏4
Other(specify)_____	❏5

(b) Since when has he/she been in this relationship (marriage, cohabitation or other)?

Since year: 19____ or

Less that 1 year ❏1	1-3 years ❏2	3-5 years ❏3
5-10 years ❏4	10-15 years ❏5	15-20 years ❏6
More that 20 years ❏7		

6. [*Answer if relationship was marriage or cohabitation: codes 1,2 or 3 at Q 5(a). Otherwise skip to Q.7*]
Record below (a) the status of the relationship when client first came for consultation and (b) the present status of the relationship. If client has a new relationship with a more recent partner, disregard here. If present marital status is unchanged from status at first consultation, tick same boxes under (a) and (b).

	(a) Status of relationship at first consultation	(b) Present status
Living together (no orders in place)	❏1	❏1
Living together, protection order in place	❏2	❏2
LIVING APART:		
Informally separated	❏3	❏3
Barring order in place	❏4	❏4
Desertion	❏5	❏5
Legally separated	❏6	❏6
Divorced in another county and not legally separated in Ireland	❏7	❏7
Church annulment and not legally separated	❏8	❏8
Other _____	❏9	❏9

7 (a) What is the client's principal source of income (tick one only)?

Own paid work	☐1
Social Welfare	☐2
Private pension	☐3
Support from co-residing spouse/partner	☐4 ——→ *Skip to Q.8*
Support from absent spouse/partner (maintenance)	☐5
Other(specify)_____	☐6

(b) About how much is the clients total take-home pay per week from all sources, net of deductions? State general range if exact information not available.

£_____ per week (if stated monthly, divide by 4 and record as weekly)

8. What is client's employment status?:

Full-time employer/self-employed	☐1	Unemployed	☐4
Full-time employee	☐2	In home duties	☐5
Part-time employer/employee	☐3	Retired	☐6
Other (specify)_____			☐7

9. If employed, unemployed or retired, what is /was clients normal principal occupation?
Job title: _____
Main duties:_____
If farmer, state size of farm:_____acres

10. (a) In what county does client live? County_____
(b) Does he/she live in: City ☐1 Town/suburb ☐2 Rural area ☐3

SECTION III. PERSONAL DETAILS OF PRINCIPAL OTHER PARTY INVOLVED

11. *Sex:* Male ☐1 Female ☐2

12. Year of birth: 19_____ *or* age group:

15-19☐1	20-24☐2	25-29☐3	30-34☐4
35-39☐5	40-44☐6	45-49☐7	50-54☐8
55-59☐9	60-64☐10	65 + ☐11	

13 (a) What is the other party's *principal* source of income (tick one only)?

Own paid work ☐1
Social Welfare ☐2
Private pension ☐3
Support from co-residing spouse/partner ☐4 ⟶ *Skip to Q.14*
Support from absent spouse/partner
　(maintenance) ☐5
Other(specify)_____ ☐6

(b) About how much is the other party's total take-home pay per week from all sources, net of deductions? State general range if exact information not available.

£_____ per week (if stated monthly, divide by 4 and record as weekly)

14. What is other party's employment status?:
Full-time employer/self-employed ☐1　Unemployed ☐4
Full-time employee ☐2　In home duties ☐5
Part-time employer/employee ☐3　Retired ☐6
Other (specify)_____ ☐7

15. If employed/self employed, unemployed or retired, what is other party's normal principal occupation?
Job title: _____
Main duties:_____
If farmer, state size of farm:_____acres

16. Has your client attended family mediation . . .
Before consulting with you?　Yes ☐1 No ☐2 Don't know ☐3
Since consulting with you?　Yes ☐1 No ☐2 Don't know ☐3

(If mediation both before and since consulting, code for both)

17. (a) When this client first came to you, who was mainly taking the initiative in bringing the case to law — your client or the other party?

Your client was the initiator, other party was responding ☐1
Other party was the initiator, your client was responding ☐2
Both were initiators, more or less to same degree ☐3
Main initiative taken by third party ☐4
Other/None of the above — *describe situation* . . . ☐5

_____
_____

(b) As of now, would you say that this case is . . .

At an early stage ☐1

Well advanced but with no immediate conclusion in sight? ☐2

Concluded, or likely to be concluded soon ☐3

18. Up to this point in this case, what issues have been "on the table" in a substantial way, whether advanced by your client or the other party? Include issues that may have been dealt with by a previous solicitor or by a family mediator, or that may have gone to court without legal representation (e.g. barring order). *Tick all that apply*

Separation agreement ☐1

Separation order ☐2

Separation order by consent ☐3

If more than one of these three items apply, tick the one which is most likely to be the final outcome.

Foreign divorce ☐4

Maintenance of spouse ☐5

Maintenance of children ☐6

Custody ☐7

Access ☐8

Property orders/agreements ☐9

Barring order ☐10

Unmarried persons only:

Paternity suit ☐11

Guardianship of children ☐12

*Other (specify)*_____

_____

19. (a) Is there a maintenance arrangement in place at present between the parties?

Yes ☐1   No ☐2 ⟶ *Skip to Q.20*

(b) [*If yes*] Was this arrangement arrived at . . .

by agreement ☐1   *or*   by judicial order ☐2

(c) Is it . . .   payable **to** your client ☐1   payable **by** your client ☐2

(d) What is the weekly amount? £_____ (*if payable monthly, divide by 4 and record as weekly*)

(e) Are the payments up to date? Yes ☐1 No ☐2 Don't know ☐3

(f) If not up to date, by how many weeks are payments in arrears?
_____weeks

(g) Has an attachment of earnings order been made in connection
with this arrangement?

Yes ❑1 No ❑2

20. (a) What kind of family home did the parties occupy together?

Privately owned with mortgage   ❑1
Privately owned, no mortgage   ❑2
Private rented   ❑3
Local authority rented   ❑4
Parties did not have their own
    family home   ❑5 ⟶ *Skip to Q.21*
Other_____

_____

(b) Has there been any legal action or negotiation concerning the
family home in the present case?

No, family home never subject of negotiation
    or action   ❑1 ⟶ *Skip to Q.21*
Yes, negotiation/action occurred by
    settlement not yet reached   ❑2 ⟶ *Skip to Q.21*
Yes, settlement reached or very likely
    to be reached   ❑3 ⟶ *Ask (c)*

(c) [*If settlement reached or likely to be reached*]. What is the
settlement . . .

(i) regarding occupancy?
    Husband moves out, wife stays   ❑1
    Wife moves out, husband stays   ❑2
    Both move out, original home disposed of ❑3
    Both stay   ❑4
    Other   ❑5

(ii) regarding ownership or financial compensation (e.g. buy-out of
one party by the other, agreement to divide proceeds of sale of
family home)?

_____
_____
_____
_____

21. (a) Have court proceedings occurred or are they likely to occur in the present case?

Yes ☐1   No ☐2

(b) *(If yes)* Have they/will they occur in the . . .

District court	☐1	
Circuit court	☐2	*If more than one,*
High court	☐3	*tick all that apply*
Other_____	☐4	

(c) Is this case . . .

Private	☐1
Civil legal aid	☐2

SECTION V. DETAILS OF CLIENT'S CHILDREN

22. (a) How many children (of any age) has client? *Include only children with partner in present case.*

_____*If none, write "none" and skip to Q.24*

(b) Record ages and residence of dependent children below — i.e. children aged under 18, or children aged 18 or over who are living with and being supported by parent(s). (If more than 6, record 6 for oldest only).

	Approximate age	Residence:
		1. Full-time with both parents 2. Mainly with mother 3. Mainly with father 4. Equally with each in turn 5. Mainly with neither
1st child		Code:_____
2nd child		Code:_____
3rd child		Code:_____
4th child		Code:_____
5th child		Code:_____
6th child		Code:_____

23. To what extent would you say that questions of custody or access concerning these children are in dispute in the legal proceedings in the present case?

Major focus of dispute	❏1
Secondary by significant focus of dispute	❏2
Minor focus of dispute	❏3
Not in dispute at all	❏4

NOTES/COMMENTS:

Appendix III

Means Test for Civil Legal Aid, 1995

This appendix sets out the means test used to determine financial eligibility for civil legal aid, as revised in 1995. A person is financially eligible if his or her disposable income and disposable capital are within certain limits.

Income Eligibility

Disposable income is the income that remains after various deductions have been made in respect of dependants, rent/mortgage, income tax, social insurance, etc. The present eligibility limit is £7,350 per annum disposable income (in 1993-94, the eligibility limit was £6,200 per annum).

Income Contribution

A person whose disposable income does not exceed £5,060 per annum is required to pay a contribution of £4 for legal advice and £23 for legal aid.

Where the disposable income exceeds £5,060 per annum, a person is required to pay a larger contribution up to a maximum of £595.

Capital

If it becomes necessary to go to Court, the value of the applicant's capital resources (e.g. house, land, money in bank, car) are also taken into account and a capital contribution may be payable. However, capital contributions arise in very few cases.

Present Allowances Against Income

The maximum allowance for the purpose of calculating the disposable income of applicants for legal services are as follows:

Applicant's spouse 1,328
Dependent child 668
Rent 2,976
Payment towards household
  expenses by unmarried persons 1,256
Mortgage 3,802
Travelling expenses 265
Hire purchase payments 265
Loan interest payments 602
Life and health insurance 754
Board and lodgings 50% of payments up to 1,599
Child care expenses 668
Income tax .... Full amount
Social insurance .... Full amount

Examples of Operation of Means Test

The following are some examples of the operation of the means test in the case of a married person with a dependent spouse and three children and certain outgoings:

Married person with 3 children on a gross income of £11,825:

Income		£11,825
Less allowances	£	£
Spouse	1,328	
3 children	2,004	
Travel expenses	265	
Rent	1,300	
P.R.S.I.	771	
P.A.Y.E.	1,627	7,295
	Disposable income	4,530
Contribution: £23		

Married person with 3 children on a gross income of £14,720:

Income			£14,720
Less allowances	£		£
Spouse	1,328		
3 children	2,004		
Travel expenses	265		
Rent	1,300		
P.R.S.I.	998		
P.A.Y.E.	2,408		8,303
		Disposable income	6,417
Contribution: £362			

Married person with 3 children on a gross income of £16,000:

Income			£16,000
Less allowances	£		£
Spouse	1,328		
3 children	2,004		
Travel expenses	265		
Rent	2,976		
P.R.S.I.	1,097		
P.A.Y.E.	2,754		10,424
		Disposable income	5,576
Contribution: £152			

Source: Legal Aid Board.

REFERENCES

Browne, D. and R. Connolly (1995) *Domestic Violence: The Response of the Legal System*. Dublin: Coolock Community Law Centre.

Duncan, W.R. and P.E. Scully (1990) *Marriage Breakdown in Ireland*. Dublin: Butterworths.

Fahey, T. (1993) "Full Citizenship for the Next Generation", in S. Healy and B. Reynolds (eds) *New Frontiers for Full Citizenship*. Dublin: Conference of Major Religious Superiors.

Goode, W.J. (1993) *World Changes in Divorce Patterns*. New Haven and London: Yale University Press.

Law Reform Commission (1994) *Consultation Paper on Family Courts*. Dublin: Law Reform Commission.

Legal Aid Board (1993) *Annual Report and Accounts 1992*. Dublin: Legal Aid Board

Marital Breakdown. A Review and Proposed Changes (Pl. 9104). Dublin: Stationery Office.

Nic Ghiolla Phádraig, M. (1992) *Marital Separation in Ireland. Situating the Results of Research on the First Three Years of Operation of the Family Mediation Service*. Dublin: Family Studies Centre, University College Dublin.

O'Connor, P.A. (1988) *Key Issues in Irish Family Law*. Dublin: Round Hall Press.

O'Higgins, K. (1974) *Marital Desertion in Dublin: An Exploratory Study*. Dublin: The Economic and Social Research Institute

Report of the Joint Oireachtas Committee on Marriage Breakdown (Pl. 3074). Dublin: Stationery Office.

Shatter, A. (1986) *Family Law in the Republic of Ireland*. (3rd Edition). Dublin: Wolfhound Press.

Ward, P. (1988) "Barring Orders: A Need for Change" *Irish Law Times,* April 1988.

Ward, P. (1990) *The Financial Consequences of Marital Breakdown*. Dublin: Combat Poverty Agency.

Ward, P. (1993) *Divorce — Who Should Bear the Costs?* Cork: Cork University Press.